A MIDSUMMER NIGHT'S DREAM

A MIDSUMMER NIGHT'S DREAM

William Shakespeare

Edited by
CEDRIC WATTS

WORDSWORTH CLASSICS

First published in 1992 by Wordsworth Editions Limited
8b East Street, Ware, Hertfordshire SG12 9HJ

ISBN 1 85326 030 4

4 6 8 10 9 7 5 3

Wordsworth® is a registered trademark of
Wordsworth Editions Limited

Typeset by Antony Gray
Printed and bound in Great Britain by
Mackays of Chatham plc, Chatham, Kent

CONTENTS

GENERAL INTRODUCTION

The Wordsworth Classics' Shakespeare Series, with *Henry V* and *The Merchant of Venice* as its inaugural volumes, presents a newly-edited sequence of William Shakespeare's works. Wordsworth Classics are inexpensive paperbacks for students and for the general reader. Each play in the Shakespeare Series is accompanied by a standard apparatus, including an introduction, explanatory notes and a glossary. The textual editing takes account of recent scholarship while giving the material a careful reappraisal. The apparatus is, however, concise rather than elaborate. We hope that the resultant volumes prove to be handy, reliable and helpful. Above all, we hope that, from Shakespeare's works, readers will derive pleasure, wisdom, provocation, challenges, and insights: insights into his culture and ours, and into the era of civilisation to which his writings have made − and continue to make − such potently influential contributions. Shakespeare's eloquence will, undoubtedly, re-echo 'in states unborn and accents yet unknown'.

CEDRIC WATTS
Series Editor

INTRODUCTION

'How shall we find the concord of this discord?'

(5.1.60.)

When Samuel Pepys saw *A Midsummer Night's Dream* in September 1662, he remarked that he had never seen it before – 'nor shall ever again, for it is the most insipid ridiculous play that ever I saw in my life'.[1] Pepys, however, appears to have been vastly outnumbered, for over the centuries *A Midsummer Night's Dream* has proved to be one of the most popular of Shakespeare's comedies, frequently revived in the theatre, and sometimes triumphantly revived there. Certainly, the play has often served mainly as the basis for free adaptations, variously operatic and spectacular; and the incidental music composed by Mendelssohn in 1843 accompanied many such versions. R. A. Foakes says that

> the habit of treating *A Midsummer Night's Dream* as a musical extravaganza, with the text often heavily cut, persisted into the twentieth century. In addition to scenic spectacles and troops [*sic*] of balletic fairies – sometimes played by women, sometimes by infants – producers often allowed their fancy to run riot in 'upholstering' the play, as in the use of electric fireflies in Augustine Daly's 1888 staging, or the innovation of a fight between a spider and a wasp in Frank Benson's treatment of it in 1889.[2]

In contrast, in 1914 Harley Granville Barker offered a controversial production which was innovatory both in its modernism and in its conservatism. It restored the full text, used an apron stage (imitating Elizabethan practice), and used male actors for Oberon and Robin (previously, these rôles had often been assigned to women).[3] But probably the most important production in the 20th Century was Peter Brook's at London in 1970: this soon became legendary for its originality, verve and vitality; it was a great success with the public and with most (though certainly not all) of its reviewers.[4] It proved that what, on the page, may appear trivial or clumsy can, in a good production, appear profound and delicate, fantastic and enchanting, eerie and erotic.

Certainly, if you want gritty realism, you'll find little of it in the text of A Midsummer Night's Dream. Instead, you find fairies, autocrats, rural buffoons, and a bizarre mixture of ancient and modern, of what is supposedly the legendary Grecian past and rural Elizabethan England. It's a surrealistic world in which the magic wielded in the inner action extends onwards and outwards to what probably was a real-life wedding. Layers on layers, worlds within worlds: there is a recessive quality created by the craftily hierarchical plotting; and at the centre of the plot is that gross breach of hierarchy, when Bottom, his head transformed into that of an ass, is embraced in moonlight by Titania, queen of immortals.

The moon is the tutelary deity of this play. In every act, the planet is present or is invoked, whether directly or indirectly – invoked more frequently than in any other Shakespeare play. In A Midsummer Night's Dream the word 'moon' is used 28 times;[5] in other plays it appears most frequently in Love's Labour's Lost (ten times), The Taming of the Shrew (eight times) and Antony and Cleopatra (again eight times). The reasons for the predominance in A Midsummer Night's Dream are evident. Most of the action takes place at night; more importantly, Shakespeare exploits thematically the moon's associations. Sometimes the moon is associated with chastity, because Diana, the lunar goddess, was the virgin huntress. (A nun will live 'a barren sister . . . , / Chanting faint hymns to the cold fruitless moon'.) Sometimes it is associated with marriage: for a traditional superstition held that the time of the new moon was a propitious time for weddings.[6] (Hippolyta assures Theseus that soon the planet 'like to a silver bow / New-bent in heaven' will shine, so that their nuptials may proceed.) Another superstition held that to sleep in moonlight might induce madness: the very word 'lunacy' connotes the influence of Luna, the moon. Theseus will equate lovers and poets with lunatics. Above all, here as in

Shakespeare's works generally, the moon, which is never stable but moves through the skies, waxing and waning, is the planet of mutability, presiding over change. The moon-goddess herself was protean, manfesting herself as Luna, Phoebe or Cynthia in the sky, Diana or Lucina on earth, and Proserpina and Hecate when in Hades or visiting the earth.[7] So this play is about metamorphoses, 'translations', transformations. Just like the 'far-off mountains turnèd into clouds', the ruthless laws which, at the beginning of the action, seem as rigid as iron are transformed, towards the end, into conventions as soft as chocolate teapots.[8] Young people who seem devoted to each other will, by enchantment, be converted into quarrelsome, angry and jealous rivals. Bottom, endearingly self-assured but sometimes asinine in character, has his head transformed into that of an ass – 'Bless thee, Bottom, bless thee! Thou art translated.' And, although the moon has presided symbolically over much of the action, it becomes demeaningly burlesqued as one of the *dramatis personae*, performed by Starveling, in the play-within-a-play, 'Pyramus and Thisby'.

Early in *A Midsummer Night's Dream*, social and conceptual hierarchies are firmly established, only to be the more strikingly breached and confused before the eventual clarifications and restoration of order. At the base of the social ladder are Bottom and his fellows; above them are the lovers, subject to the intended control of Egeus and the jurisdiction of Theseus; and beyond them, as influential observers and manipulators, are proud Oberon and his henchman, Robin. Shakespeare was no socialist and hardly a democrat (indeed, you'd have difficulty in finding one in his era),[9] but there's plenty to gratify one's sense of sympathy with the under-dog. The 'Pyramus and Thisby' drama may predictably collapse into buffoonish farce; yet, from the point of view of theatre audiences, it is usually a comic peak of the action: Bottom and Company are more successful than they ever realise. Their play about tragic misreadings of the situation makes an ironic commentary on the misreadings and misunderstandings that have taken place in the action involving the fugitive lovers. Bottom is treated derisively by Oberon and Robin; but he has the last laugh. Converted into an ass-headed grotesque who delights the deluded Titania, he enjoys bliss with her in her bower. Whether that bliss seems sexual, non-sexual, or sexual-and-more will depend on your interpretation of the text and/or on the nature of the production that you see. Peter Brook's production made the central moment of the play the ecstatic joy as the tumescent Bottom was carried aloft with Titania in an opulently crimson-feathered bed: no doubt about it, sexual orgasm was imminent.[10] But when Bottom later tries to recall the event, it is already a dream dissolving and fading from memory: he captures only a sense of the wondrous and ineffable.

> I have had a dream – past the wit of man to say what dream it was. Man is but an ass, if he go about to expound this dream. Methought I was – there is no man can tell what. Methought I was, and methought I had . . . But man is but a patched fool, if he will offer to say what methought I had.

So, at the centre of the action, lies a lacuna and an enigma: an undefined union of a beautiful immortal with a buffoonish mortal wearing an ass's head, in a glorious breach of hierarchy. Oberon thought he was punishing Titania, but it makes the play morally better if we think that Oberon has been cuckolded by Bottom. Both Titania and Bottom are, at the time, subject to the magic inflicted on them by Oberon via Robin; therefore, if the couple, instead of suffering the intended humiliation, enjoy an extreme of bliss, that serves Oberon and Robin right. There's no need to worry about whether the bliss was sexual *or* innocent, for that seems to be a false disjunction in this case: it's not a matter of 'either/or' but of, at least, 'both/and'. 'Mortal grossness' has been sublimated.

One of the most attractive features of the play is its combination of fantasy and common sense, of airy feyness and solid substance. When the beautiful Titania falls in love with the transmogrified Bottom, the fantastic event evokes a familiar reality. 'I wonder what she sees in him?' is a remark sometimes heard at a wedding, and 'He's making an ass of himself' can sometimes be heard at a reception. Desire indeed unites strange bed-fellows and reminds us of legendary incongruities. In ancient legend, Midas's ears became those of an ass; Circe, the seductive enchantress, turned men into swine; and Apuleius's Lucius became an asinine sexual athlete. Such stories illustrate the perennial recognition that the borderline between the human and the bestial is shifting and variable. People's sexual desires and appetites can subvert reason and may result in exultation, but they may also reveal our kinship with brutes. Shakespeare's variation on this theme, in the person of Bottom, suggests not only a metaphor made literal (this man 'is but an ass' in his imperturbable folly; the asinine head offers a tangible representation of the intangible quality), but also the possibility of a transcendent rather than a demeaning experience: desire may open a gateway to the ineffable. If we look at the confusions of Hermia, Lysander, Helena and Demetrius (those confusions induced when Robin drips the drug into the wrong person's eyes), we see that what is given comic acceleration and heightening is, yet again, a familiar truth: love is fickle; lovers may vehemently swear constancy, but all too often infidelities ensue. While extolling the uniqueness of their particular objects of desire, people in love behave predictably and interchangeably. Ultimately, in the play, the artificially-induced confusion is artificially resolved; the course of true love does eventually seem to run smooth. But what has been presented in comic and even farcical form is a perennial reality which may bear tragic consequences. In addition, as Judith Buchanan remarks, the flow of action contains undercurrents of violence:

> [M]ost of the acts, or threatened acts, of aggression in the play are committed by men on women (Theseus' wooing of Hippolyta with his sword, Egeus' insistent call for the death of his own daughter, Oberon's desire to exact physical and psychological revenge on Titania, Demetrius' rape threat to Helena) . . . [11]

Titania, in turn, is quite prepared to hold Bottom captive – and a gagged captive at that: 'Tie up my love's tongue: bring him silently'. The very climate of the region has (we are told) been thrown into turmoil by the dissension between Oberon and Titania. Modes of disruption and aggression precede the eventual assurance that 'all shall be well' and the reconciliation of the differing groups.

The characters in *A Midsummer Night's Dream* are, of course, bizarrely diverse. We encounter (among others): a king and queen of the fairies who control the climate; a puck (a kind of goblin) and lesser fairies of variable sizes (some being too minute to be accurately represented on stage); rustics who seem to be denizens of the rural England of Shakespeare's day; a 'duke' who rules Athens and is supposed to be the heroic Theseus of ancient Greek legend; and his fiancée, who is a queen of the mythical Amazons. The allusions span thousands of years: Hecate, Cupid, Diana, Hercules, Ariadne, Corin, Phillida, English folk-lore, nuns in convents, the nine-men's morris, a fowler firing his gun at choughs. The flora and fauna evoke Shakespeare's Warwickshire far more than legendary Attica, but nevertheless include lions and apes. The weather is supposed to be in a state of oppressive turmoil, with fields flooded in summer; yet the night depicted is so clement that lovers can sleep in the open air. Robin imposes a fog on mortals, but later becomes their floor-sweeper. Culturally, geographically, chronologically and meteorologically, therefore, the play might appear so muddled as to strain credulity to breaking-point. In practice, it is this very muddle that yields much of the pleasure: customary categories are breached, confused and blended; metamorphoses are at work in our mental filing-systems; logic takes a holiday; and finally in the play there is a partial restoration of the familiar which leaves an enduring sense of its partial subversion.

One of the most memorable, and memorably-ironic, speeches in the whole of Shakespeare is uttered by Theseus in the final act:

> I never may believe
> These antique fables, nor these fairy toys.
> Lovers and madmen have such seething brains,
> Such shaping fantasies, that apprehend
> More than cool reason ever comprehends.
> The lunatic, the lover and the poet
> Are of imagination all compáct.
> One sees more devils than vast hell can hold:
> That is the madman. The lover, all as frantic,
> Sees Helen's beauty in a brow of Egypt.
> The poet's eye, in a fine frenzy rolling,
> Doth glance from heaven to earth, from earth to heaven;
> And as imagination bodies forth
> The forms of things unknown, the poet's pen
> Turns them to shapes, and gives to airy nothing

> A local habitation and a name.
> Such tricks hath strong imagination
> That, if it would but apprehend some joy,
> It comprehends some bringer of that joy;
> Or in the night, imagining some fear,
> How easy is a bush supposed a bear!

One obvious function of this speech is to vent scepticism – not just the character's, but the audience's lurking scepticism, which here finds voice in Theseus's words. 'Antique fables, . . . fairy toys': that's what anyone might think on reading a plot-summary of *A Midsummer Night's Dream*. According to Theseus, both the poet and the lover are no better than the lunatic: all three let imagination prevail over reality. The lover, deluded fellow, thinks that a swarthy gypsy is as beautiful as Helen of Troy; the poet gives shape to 'airy nothings': thus both are deranged; and all are no better than the fearful night-walker who thinks a bush is a bear. If, however, the scepticism of Theseus (together with the element of scepticism haunting the audience's response to the play) here gains expression, it does so in order to be subverted ironically. In the first place, who is saying this? Why, the fictional Theseus, who had once been personally aided by the Queen of Fairies; an imaginary hero, product of a poet (and of many story-tellers in the past), and here played by an actor. So, the more convincingly authoritative the Duke's words seem, the more thoroughly they are mocked by the situation. In Theseus' world, immortals intermingle with mortals; and, if lovers' delusions have been portrayed, they are delusions which we (deluded into suspending some disbelief) have watched with sympathy as well as amusement. As Hippolyta says, the lovers' stories seem consistent, expressing 'something of great constancy', and, moreover, something 'strange and admirable' – unfamiliar and to be wondered at, not dismissed. In that respect, Bottom's response was wiser than Theseus's.

> The eye of man hath not heard, the ear of man hath not seen, man's hand is not able to taste, his tongue to conceive, nor his heart to report, what my dream was.

Whereas Theseus is reductively dismissive, Bottom in these

words recognises the reality of experiences which transcend expression and comprehension. His phrasing involves muddled recollection of I Corinthians 2:9–10:

> The eye hath not seen, and the ear hath not heard, neither have entered into the heart of man, the things which God hath prepared for them that love him.
> But God hath opened them unto us by his spirit. For the spirit searcheth all things, yea the bottom of God's secrets.[12]

Bottom himself is clearly the appropriate person to plumb secrets to their bottom. He certainly hasn't plumbed *God*'s secrets, for the fantasia in which he is involved has a predominantly non-Christian metaphysic; but his muddled phrasing is a way of conveying an experience that eluded words. Indeed, the very muddle – expressing a synaesthesia or confusion of the senses – is entirely apt in this play of metamorphoses and confusions. The changes and entanglements are present not only at the level of plot and characterisation but also here, for a moment, at the level of the very vocabulary: so his comic malapropisms briefly glow with symbolism. Instead of giving to 'airy nothing' a 'local habitation and a name', Bottom has evoked 'airy something' by his failure to define a recollection. Of course, Theseus, in the very act of denigrating the poet as a mere fantasist, had uttered splendid lines of poetry, rhetorically resonant, rhythmically cumulative, and sensuously seductive in the patterns of alliteration and assonance. As elsewhere in the play, Shakespeare delights in conceptual paradox.

A paradox of a kind that frequently occurs in his plays is found in the epilogue, when the audience is addressed by a Robin who is a speaking 'shadow', simultaneously the fictional puck and an actor appealing for applause for the show. He becomes a hybrid entity, part fantasy and part substance, rather as Bottom was a mixture of ass and man. He points out that the performance may be treated by any discontented patrons as a communal – and inconsequential – dream. The postulate that the play may be 'inconsequential' has been amply refuted by cultural history, for its theatrical and critical 'consequences' continue to this day; and, in both the world of the theatre and the arena of critical wrangling, the prestige of *A Midsummer Night's Dream* continues to grow. The continuing attraction, as so often with Shakespeare's works, lies partly in our sense of homage to the past, in maintenance of a tradition which displays respect for our ancestors' customs and values. It is a democratic homage: we pay respect to the silent majority, our dead predecessors, as well as to an eloquent minority of superb writers of whom Shakespeare is the leader. But there is also the appeal of understanding the present by trying to bring the present into critical relationship with the past. If film-makers or stage-directors and actors successfully take liberties with this play, the effect may be that of 'love-in-idleness' in the beholders' eyes, transforming the vision. Shakespeare, so often difficult and puzzling, may be rendered our contemporary again, re-energised by contemporary imaginations.

Shakespeare may not have been a democrat, but he could be proleptic, looking ahead and helping to effect cultural changes. One of the most movingly proleptic speeches in the play occurs when Theseus is warned that the drama which Bottom and his company intend to present will be too crude for enjoyment. Theseus says that what matters is the 'simpleness and duty' of the offering. He then elaborates on this theme:

> Where I have come, great clerks have purposèd
> To greet me with premeditated welcomes;
> Where I have seen them shiver and look pale,
> Make periods in the midst of sentences,
> Throttle their practised accent in their fears,
> And in conclusion dumbly have broke off,
> Not paying me a welcome. Trust me, sweet,
> Out of this silence, yet, I picked a welcome,
> And in the modesty of fearful duty
> I read as much as from the rattling tongue
> Of saucy and audacious eloquence.
> Love, therefore, and tongue-tied simplicity,
> In least, speak most, to my capacity.

This puts to shame Oberon and Robin, who had treated with patronising contempt the 'crew of patches, rude mechanicals', among whom Bottom seemed '[t]he shallowest thick-skin of that barren sort'. Theseus (even if he later laughs at the show) here gives the immortals a moral lesson; indeed, Shakespeare was simultaneously giving his contemporaries a lesson in courtesy, gentlemanliness and considerately civilised conduct. It's one of those literary speeches which help – albeit tricklingly and imperceptibly – to make the world a better place. Shakespeare was a sophisticated observer and demonstrator of modes of courtesy, a topic that held little interest for his greatest contemporaries, Marlowe and Jonson. Harold Brooks speculates that Queen Elizabeth may have been present when the play was first performed, and that this speech may have been designed as a compliment to her known magnanimity when being welcomed and entertained.[13] Various commentators have assumed that the 'imperial vot'ress', the 'fair vestal, thronèd by the west,' who has eluded Cupid's arrow (in Act 2, scene 1), is Elizabeth, the Virgin Queen.[14]

A related – though disputed – contextual possibility is that *A Midsummer Night's Dream* was written to grace a noble wedding (perhaps attended by the Queen). It's not unusual for a comedy to culminate in one or more weddings; but this play gives special emphasis to the culmination of the action in multiple wedlock. Furthermore, the close of Act 5, when Oberon, Titania and Robin pronounce elaborate blessing on the house (or 'palace'), on its owner, its bride-bed, the newly-weds and their children to come, strongly suggests that the play was first performed at some stately home in which a marriage was being celebrated. Some commentators think that the occasion was the wedding of Elizabeth Carey and Thomas, the son of Henry, Lord Berkeley, on 19 February 1596. 'It evidently took place from the mansion of the bride's father, Sir George Carey, in Blackfriars', says Brooks.[15] Her grandfather was Lord Hunsdon, the Lord Chamberlain, patron of Shakespeare's company of players. (When the aged patron died in July of that year, Sir George became Lord Chamberlain in turn.) The elegant, courtly, patrician features of the play would be appropriate to such an occasion, though the script may well have been modified by Shakespeare afterwards for the various public performances which evidently ensued. Thus, when Bottom and his friends stage their drama to grace a wedding, they may be offering a parody of what Shakespeare and his colleagues were originally doing.[16]

In any case, Shakespeare thought dialectically: he relished mutually-enhancing contrasts. Against the courtliness of the play, there's the farce of the 'Pyramus and Thisby' drama within it. Against the quarrels and recriminations of the lovers, there's the lyrical poetry of natural beauty, as when Oberon says:

> I know a bank whereon the wild thyme blows,
> Where oxlips and the nodding violet grows,
> Quite over-canopied with luscious woodbine,
> With sweet musk-roses, and with eglantine . . .

This is the kind of sensuous descriptive verse that the Romantic Movement was to imitate and amplify in a thousand odes and ballads: indeed, the violet, musk-rose and eglantine in Keats's 'Ode to a Nightingale' probably sprang not from the soil but from the pages of A Midsummer Night's Dream.[17] But even within the rural poetry of Shakespeare's play there is a range of contrasts, extending from fantasy to reminders of mundane labour. For lyrical fantasy, there's the fairy's service of Titania, seeking dew-drops 'to hang a pearl in every cowslip's ear'; and, in contrast, there's the claim that it's Robin who sabotages rural toil, depriving milk of its cream, so that 'the breathless housewife' churns fruitlessly. Theseus says that the poet's eye 'doth glance from heaven to earth, from earth to heaven'. In A Midsummer Night's Dream, Shakespeare's eye, similarly, perceives the transcendent and the mundane, the delicate and the earthy, the poignant and the bawdy, creating a shimmering fantasia which yet derives from familiar experience; creating, from discord, concord.

NOTES TO THE INTRODUCTION

1 The Diary of Samuel Pepys, ed. Robert Latham and William Matthews, Vol. 3 (London: Bell, 1970), p. 208. Pepys admitted that he saw there 'some good dancing and some handsome women'.

2 'Introduction' to A Midsummer Night's Dream, ed. R. A. Foakes (Cambridge: Cambridge University Press, 1984), pp. 15–16. (Foakes's 'troops' should be 'troupes'.)

3 This production by Granville Barker (who later hyphenated these two names) is described in J. L. Styan's The Shakespeare Revolution (Cambridge: Cambridge University Press, 1977), pp. 95–104.

4 The Peter Brook production is described in *The Shakespeare Revolution*, pp. 224–31. A very detailed account of the rehearsals is David Selbourne's *The Making of 'A Midsummer Night's Dream'* (London: Methuen, 1982).

5 This is without counting such compounds as 'moonlight' and 'moonshine'.

6 See *A Dictionary of Superstitions*, ed. Iona Opie and Moira Tatem (Oxford: Oxford University Press, 1989), pp. 261–2.

7 In Act 5, scene 1, Robin says that he and other fairies run alongside Hecate's chariot. Incidentally, his claim that they 'run / . . . From the presence of the sun, / Following darkness' seems to contradict Oberon's 'But we are spirits of another sort' (i.e. not night-creatures) in Act 3, scene 2.

8 In Act 1, scene 1, Theseus says that he can 'by no means...extenuate' the stern laws which Egeus has evoked; but in Act 4, scene 1, he peremptorily declares: 'Egeus, I will overbear your will.' The ending of a comedy often entails the defeat of logic by form.

9 Tellingly, the original (Q1) stage-direction at the opening of what is now Act 4, scene 2, reads '*Enter Flute, Thisbe and the rabble*'. Editors usually regard this direction as Shakespeare's.

10 I'm referring to the performance that I saw (with delight) one day in 1970. Stagings of this part of Brook's production varied, but they left no doubt that sexual bliss was impending. Although some editors of the play deny that copulation takes place between Bottom and Titania, their view was definitely not shared by Brook.

11 'Introduction' to William Shakespeare: *Four Great Comedies* (Ware: Wordsworth Editions, 1998), p. 11. Jan Kott, in *Shakespeare Our Contemporary*, had emphasised or postulated violent aspects of the play.

12 I quote the translation (1525–6) by William Tyndale (*Tyndale's New Testament*: modern-spelling edition by David Daniell; New Haven and London: Yale University Press, 1989).

13 'Introduction' to *A Midsummer Night's Dream*, ed. Harold F. Brooks (London: Methuen, 1979), p. lv.

14 John Dover Wilson sceptically observed, however: '[W]e are not convinced that the lines would have been taken as complimentary by the Queen . . . [E]ven maiden ladies of ordinary rank are apt to be touchy about references to past courtships.' See *A Midsummer Night's Dream*, ed. Sir Arthur Quiller-Couch and John Dover Wilson (London: Cambridge University Press, 1924, rpt. 1969), p. 116.

15 Brooks, p. lvi.

16 I think that the original occasion may well have been a noble wedding; but there is no firm evidence to show that it was that of Elizabeth

Carey. For a sceptical view of the 'noble wedding' theory, see 'Introduction' to *A Midsummer Night's Dream*, ed. Peter Holland (Oxford: Oxford University Press, 1994), pp. 111–12. Incidentally, whereas Brooks suggests that the Carey wedding took place 'from' the family mansion, Buchanan suggests that it took place 'at' the family mansion.

17 See stanza 5 of Keats's ode.

FURTHER READING
(in chronological order)

C. L. Barber: *Shakespeare's Festive Comedy*. Princeton, N, J.: Princeton University Press; London: Oxford University Press; 1959.

Jan Kott: *Shakespeare Our Contemporary*. London: Methuen, 1965.

David P. Young: *Something of Great Constancy: The Art of 'A Midsummer Night's Dream'*. New Haven and London: Yale University Press, 1966.

Stephen Fender: *Shakespeare: 'A Midsummer Night's Dream'*. London: Arnold, 1968.

Shakespearian Comedy (Stratford-upon-Avon Studies, 14), ed. Malcolm Bradbury and David Palmer. London: Arnold, 1972.

Alexander Leggatt: *Shakespeare's Comedy of Love*. London and New York: Methuen, 1974.

J. L. Styan: *The Shakespeare Revolution*. Cambridge: Cambridge University Press, 1977.

Samuel Schoenbaum: *William Shakespeare: A Compact Documentary Life*. London and New York: Oxford University Press, 1977, rpt. 1987.

David Selbourne: *The Making of 'A Midsummer Night's Dream'*. London: Methuen, 1982.

Terry Eagleton: *William Shakespeare*. Oxford: Blackwell, 1986.

The Cambridge Companion to Shakespeare Studies, ed. Stanley Wells. Cambridge: Cambridge University Press, 1986.

Longman Critical Essays: 'A Midsummer Night's Dream', ed. Linda Cookson and Bryan Loughrey. Harlow: Longman, 1991.

Shakespeare's Comedies, ed. Gary Waller. Harlow: Longman, 1991.

Brian Vickers: *Appropriating Shakespeare: Contemporary Critical Quarrels*. New Haven and London: Yale University Press, 1993.

Russ McDonald: *The Bedford Companion to Shakespeare*. New York: St Martin's Press; Basingstoke: Macmillan; 1996.

Helen Hackett: *A Midsummer Night's Dream*. Plymouth: Northcote House, 1997.

Kenneth S. Rothwell: *Shakespeare on Screen: A Century of Film and Television*. Cambridge: Cambridge University Press, 1999.

John Sutherland and Cedric Watts: *Henry V, War Criminal? and Other Shakespeare Puzzles*. Oxford: Oxford University Press, 2000.

NOTE ON SHAKESPEARE

Details of Shakespeare's early life are scanty. He was the son of a prosperous merchant of Stratford-upon-Avon, and tradition gives his date of birth as 23 April, 1564; certainly, three days later, he was christened at the parish church. It is likely that he attended the local Grammar School but had no university education. Of his early career there is no record, though John Aubrey states that he was a country schoolmaster. In 1582 Shakespeare married Anne Hathaway, with whom he had two daughters, Susanna and Judith, and a son, Hamnet, who died in 1596. How he became involved with the stage in London is uncertain, but he was sufficiently established as a playwright by 1592 to be criticised in print as a challengingly versatile 'upstart Crow'. He was a leading member of the Lord Chamberlain's company, which became the King's Men on the accession of James I in 1603. Being not only a playwright and actor but also a 'sharer' (one of the owners of the company, entitled to a share of the profits), Shakespeare prospered greatly, as is proven by the numerous records of his financial transactions. Towards the end of his life, he loosened his ties with London and retired to New Place, the large property in Stratford which he had bought in 1597. He died on 23 April, 1616, and is buried in the place of his baptism, Holy Trinity Church. The earliest collected edition of his plays, the First Folio, was published in 1623, and its prefatory verse-tributes include Ben Jonson's famous declaration, 'He was not of an age, but for all time'.

ACKNOWLEDGEMENTS AND TEXTUAL MATTERS

I have consulted, and am indebted to, numerous editions of *A Midsummer Night's Dream*, notably those by: Sir Arthur Quiller-Couch and John Dover Wilson (London: Cambridge University Press, 1924, reprinted 1969); Harold F. Brooks (the Arden Shakespeare: London, Methuen, 1979); R. A. Foakes (Cambridge: Cambridge University Press, 1984); John F. Andrew (London: Dent Everyman, 1993); and Peter Holland (Oxford: Oxford University Press, 1994, reprinted 1998). The Glossary adapts and revises Dover Wilson's.

A Midsummer Night's Dream was written in or around 1595, and apparently it was 'sundry times publickely acted' before the appearance in 1600 of the first printed text, the First Quarto (Q1). This quarto is thought to have been based on Shakespeare's 'foul papers', an untidy manuscript of the play. The Second Quarto (Q2), set from Q1, appeared in 1619, though it was falsely dated '1600' to get the printer out of legal difficulties. It has various small differences from Q1 (notably, corrections of some obvious printing errors) but none that indicates any Shakespearian input. Next, the play appeared in the First Folio of 1623 (F1), the first 'Collected Edition' of Shakespeare's works. This volume was prepared by two of Shakespeare's colleagues, John Heminges and Henry Condell, and appeared seven years after Shakespeare's death. The play in F1 was set from Q2 with some reference to theatrical practice and/or to a prompt-book (the copy used by the prompter or stage-manager). It includes various substantive changes and more than thirty additional stage-directions. Q1 has no Act or scene divisions; F1 has no scene divisions. Later Folio editions (1632, 1663, etc.) make small changes to *A Midsummer*

Night's Dream, but do not incorporate any material which can be attributed to Shakespeare.

Modern editors of *A Midsummer Night's Dream* generally make a compromise between the following three elements. First, the material (sometimes divergent) in the earliest printed texts, particularly those of 1600 and 1623. Secondly, what Shakespeare is thought to have intended (which sometimes differs from what those texts provide). Thirdly, modern conventions of spelling, punctuation and presentation.

My general rule has been to follow as closely as seems reasonable the text of Q1, supplemented by what seem to be authoritative changes found in F1; but, obviously, what seems reasonable to one reader may not seem so to another. If you compare different modern editions, you find predictable variations in punctuation (as the punctuation of the early texts is sometimes inadequate), in the spelling of numerous problematic words, and in the stage directions. You will also find some striking discrepancies, notably in Act 5. I'll give you, now, two examples of these.

In the 1979 Arden text edited by Harold Brooks, during what is now Act 5, scene 1, there is a sequence of dialogue in which Theseus discusses with Philostrate, his 'usual manager of mirth', the entertainments that have been proposed. In the 1994 Oxford text edited by Peter Holland, however, Philostrate has vanished from this scene: his words are now spoken by Egeus, while the titles of the proposed performances are re-allocated from Theseus to Lysander. What has happened is that the former editor has followed Q1, while the latter has followed F1. So which is preferable? The changes in F1 may have been intended as an economy by the acting company, an attempt to eliminate the actor needed for Philostrate (who previously had made only a brief appearance, in Act 1). Nevertheless, these changes introduce inconsistencies, because Egeus, the crusty father of Hermia, is an unlikely sudden choice as Master of Revels; and he is certainly not the 'usual manager of mirth', for, in Act 1, it was Philostrate who had been commanded by Theseus to arrange 'merriments'. Furthermore, perhaps as a result of a misreading by the compositor, one of the speeches in the Act 5 sequence is still attributed to Philostrate instead of being re-allocated. It does not follow, however, that editors who prefer F1 are 'wrong'. Peter Holland argues that the redistribution of words to Egeus and Lysander in this sequence enriches the characterisation and themes of the play. Nevertheless, in the present Wordsworth text, I have preferred to follow Q1, which in this matter seems consistent, logical and somewhat more authoritative.

The second example may be called 'The Mystery of the Vanishing Song'. In the closing minutes of the play, Oberon instructs the fairies to sing a 'ditty' after him and to dance 'trippingly'. Titania then says that the fairy singers will 'bless this place'. Next, Oberon, in the speech beginning 'Now, until the break of day', predicts and pronounces an elaborate blessing on the palace, its newlyweds and the owner. But where are the words of the song – or songs? Q1 does not supply them. Dr Johnson, long ago, thought that two songs were implied, even though their words were not provided: one introduced by Oberon and another introduced by Titania. In F1, however, Oberon's 'Now, until the break of day' speech is preceded by the heading '*The Song*'. Some editors, therefore, assume that this solves the problem and that his ensuing words are really the lyric. The snag here is that Oberon's speech does not resemble the normal Shakespearian lyric: it lacks a distinctive stanza-form and refrain. Quite likely, F1's heading results from a compositor's misreading of a prompt-book reference to a song. In this Wordsworth edition, I take the view that Oberon and Titania introduce one lyric, not two, and that its words are lacking. What, therefore, should be supplied in performance? In 1912, Granville Barker ingeniously filled the gap by deploying there the song which, at the beginning of the later play *The Two Noble Kinsmen*, blesses a wedding – the nuptials of (by lucky coincidence) Theseus and Hippolyta. That, you may agree, is the most elegant solution. Accordingly I provide, in the notes on the text, the words of that song.

In short, there is more 'play' – flexibility, variability and adaptability – in *A Midsummer Night's Dream* than you might at first imagine. If you compare a couple of modern texts with each other, and compare either of them with the Q1 and F1 versions, you soon realise that the options for readers, critics, actors and directors are admirably numerous. My annotations indicate a range of those options. One reason for Shakespeare's durability is that the gaps, ambiguities and puzzles in the early texts provide plenty of room for later variations, adaptations and interpretations. The more the merrier, perhaps.

I hope that the present edition of *A Midsummer Night's Dream* represents a useful compromise between the early texts, Shakespeare's intentions (so far as they can be reasonably inferred) and modern requirements. You will see that I have preserved some archaic spellings which contribute significantly to euphony or punning; but the glossary explains such words. In any case, as you read the play, you will find that to some extent you are editing it to suit yourself, even as you are directing it in your imagination.

A MIDSUMMER NIGHT'S DREAM

Scene: Athens, and a wood nearby.

CHARACTERS IN THE PLAY

OBERON, *King of Fairies.*

TITANIA, *Queen of Fairies.*

ROBIN GOODFELLOW, *a puck.*

PEASEBLOSSOM, COBWEB, MOTH *and*
MUSTARDSEED, *fairies serving Titania.*

Other FAIRIES.

THESEUS, *Duke of Athens.*

HYPPOLITA, *Queen of the Amazons.*

EGEUS, *father of Hermia.*

HERMIA, *in love with Lysander.*

LYSANDER, *in love with Hermia.*

DEMETRIUS, *suitor to Hermia.*

HELENA, *in love with Demetrius.*

PHILOSTRATE, *Theseus' Master of the Revels.*

Theseus' LORDS *and other* ATTENDANTS.

PETER QUINCE, *a carpenter.*

NICK BOTTOM, *a weaver.*

FRANCIS FLUTE, *a bellows-mender.*

TOM SNOUT, *a tinker.*

SNUG, *a joiner.*

ROBIN STARVELING, *a tailor.*

A MIDSUMMER NIGHT'S DREAM

ACT I, SCENE I.

The hall in the palace of Theseus, Duke of Athens.

Enter THESEUS *and* HIPPOLYTA,[1]
followed by PHILOSTRATE *and* ATTENDANTS.

THESEUS   Now, fair Hippolyta, our nuptial hour
Draws on apace: four happy days bring in
Another moon: but O, methinks how slow
This old moon wanes![2] She lingers my desires,
Like to a step-dame, or a dowager,
Long withering out a young man's revenue.

HIPPOLYTA   Four days will quickly steep themselves in night:
Four nights will quickly dream away the time:
And then the moon, like to a silver bow
New-bent[3] in heaven, shall behold the night   10
Of our solemnities.

THESEUS   Go, Philostrate,
Stir up the Athenian youth to merriments,
Awake the pert and nimble spirit of mirth,
Turn melancholy forth to funerals:
The pale companion is not for our pomp.

                      [*Exit Philostrate.*

Hippolyta, I wooed thee with my sword,
And won thy love, doing thee injuries;
But I will wed thee in another key,
With pomp, with triumph, and with revelling.

Enter EGEUS *and his daughter* HERMIA,
followed by LYSANDER *and* DEMETRIUS.

EGEUS   Happy be Theseus, our renownèd duke!   20

THESEUS   Thanks, good Egeus. What's the news with thee?

EGEUS   Full of vexation come I, with complaint
Against my child, my daughter Hermia.
Stand forth, Demetrius. My noble lord,
This man hath my consent to marry her.
Stand forth, Lysander. And, my gracious duke,

This man hath bewitched the bosom of my child.[4]
Thou, thou, Lysander, thou hast given her rhymes,
And interchanged love-tokens with my child;
Thou hast, by moonlight, at her window sung,   30
With feigning voice, verses of faining love,
And stol'n the impression of her fantasy[5]
With bracelets of thy hair, rings, gauds, conceits,
Knacks, trifles, nosegays, sweetmeats (messengers
Of strong prevailment in unhardened youth).
With cunning hast thou filched my daughter's heart,
Turned her obedience (which is due to me)
To stubborn harshness. And, my gracious duke,
Be it so she will not here, before your grace,
Consent to marry with Demetrius,   40
I beg the ancient privilege of Athens:
As she is mine, I may dispose of her:
Which shall be either to this gentleman,
Or to her death; according to our law
Immediately provided in that case.

THESEUS   What say you, Hermia? Be advised, fair maid.
To you, your father should be as a god:
One that composed your beauties; yea, and one
To whom you are but as a form in wax,
By him imprinted, and within his power   50
To leave the figure or disfigure it.
Demetrius is a worthy gentleman.

HERMIA   So is Lysander.

THESEUS   In himself he is;
But in this kind, wanting your father's voice,
The other must be held the worthier.

HERMIA   I would my father looked but with my eyes.

THESEUS   Rather your eyes must with his judgement look.

HERMIA   I do entreat your grace to pardon me.
I know not by what power I am made bold;
Nor how it may concern my modesty   60
In such a presence here to plead my thoughts:
But I beseech your grace that I may know
The worst that may befall me in this case,
If I refuse to wed Demetrius.

THESEUS Either to die the death, or to abjure
         For ever the society of men.
         Therefore, fair Hermia, question your desires,
         Know of your youth, examine well your blood,
         Whether (if you yield not to·your father's choice)
         You can endure the livery of a nun,   70
         For aye to be in shady cloister mewed,
         To live a barren sister all your life,
         Chanting faint hymns to the cold fruitless moon.
         Thrice blessèd they that master so their blood
         To undergo such maiden pilgrimage;
         But earthlier happy is the rose distilled,
         Than that which, withering on the virgin thorn,
         Grows, lives and dies in single blessedness.[6]

HERMIA   So will I grow, so live, so die, my lord,
         Ere I will yield my virgin patent up   80
         Unto his lordship, whose unwishèd yoke
         My soul consents not to give sovereignty.

THESEUS Take time to pause, and by the next new moon –
         The sealing-day betwixt my love and me
         For everlasting bond of fellowship –
         Upon that day either prepare to die
         For disobedience to your father's will,
         Or else to wed Demetrius, as he would,
         Or on Diana's altar to protest,
         For aye, austerity and single life.[7]   90

DEMETR. Relent, sweet Hermia; and, Lysander, yield
         Thy crazèd title to my certain right.

LYSANDER You have her father's love, Demetrius;
         Let me have Hermia's: do you marry him.

EGEUS   Scornful Lysander! True, he hath my love;
         And what is mine my love shall render him.
         And she is mine, and all my right of her
         I do estate unto Demetrius.

LYSANDER I am, my lord, as well derived as he,
         As well possessed; my love is more than his;   100
         My fortunes every way as fairly ranked
         (If not with vantage) as Demetrius';
         And which is more than all these boasts can be –

I am beloved of beauteous Hermia.
Why should not I then prosecute my right?
Demetrius — I'll avouch it to his head —
Made love to Nedar's daughter, Helena,
And won her soul; and she (sweet lady) dotes,
Devoutly dotes, dotes in idolatry,
Upon this spotted and inconstant man.   110

THESEUS   I must confess that I have heard so much,
And with Demetrius thought to have spoke thereof;
But, being over-full of self-affairs,
My mind did lose it. But, Demetrius, come,
And come, Egeus: you shall go with me:
I have some private schooling for you both.
For you, fair Hermia, look you arm yourself
To fit your fancies to your father's will;
Or else the law of Athens yields you up
(Which by no means we may extenuate)   120
To death, or to a vow of single life.
Come, my Hippolyta: what cheer, my love?
Demetrius and Egeus, go along:
I must employ you in some business[8]
Against our nuptial, and confer with you
Of something nearly that concerns yourselves.

EGEUS   With duty and desire we follow you.

                          [*Exeunt all except Hermia and Lysander.*

LYSANDER How now, my love? Why is your cheek so pale?
How chance the roses there do fade so fast?

HERMIA   Belike for want of rain, which I could well   130
Beteem them from the tempest of my eyes.

LYSANDER Ay me! For aught that I could ever read,
Could ever hear by tale or history,
The course of true love never did run smooth;
But either it was different in blood —

HERMIA   O cross! Too high to be enthralled to low.

LYSANDER Or else misgraffèd in respect of years —

HERMIA   O spite! Too old to be engaged to young.

LYSANDER Or else it stood upon the choice of friends —

HERMIA   O hell! To choose love by another's eyes!   140

LYSANDER Or, if there were a sympathy in choice,

          War, death, or sickness did lay siege to it –
          Making it momentany as a sound,
          Swift as a shadow, short as any dream,
          Brief as the lightning in the collied night
          That (in a spleen) unfolds both heaven and earth,
          And, ere a man hath power to say 'Behold!',
          The jaws of darkness do devour it up:
          So quick bright things come to confusion.[9]

HERMIA   If then true lovers have been ever crossed,   150
          It stands as an edíct in destiny:
          Then let us teach our trial patience,[10]
          Because it is a customary cross,
          As due to love as thoughts and dreams and sighs,
          Wishes and tears, poor fancy's followers.

LYSANDER A good persuasion: therefore hear me, Hermia:
          I have a widow aunt, a dowager
          Of great revénue, and she hath no child –
          From Athens is her house remote seven leagues –
          And she respects me as her only son.   160
          There, gentle Hermia, may I marry thee;
          And to that place the sharp Athenian law
          Cannot pursue us. If thou lov'st me, then,
          Steal forth thy father's house tomorrow night:
          And in the wood a league without the town
          (Where I did meet thee once with Helena
          To do observance to a morn of May),[11]
          There will I stay for thee.

HERMIA   My good Lysander,
          I swear to thee by Cupid's strongest bow,
          By his best arrow with the golden head,   170
          By the simplicity of Venus' doves,
           By that which knitteth souls and prospers loves,
          And by that fire which burned the Carthage queen,
          When the false Troyan under sail was seen,[12]
          By all the vows that ever men have broke
          (In number more than ever women spoke),
          In that same place thou hast appointed me,
          Tomorrow truly will I meet with thee.

LYSANDER Keep promise, love. Look, here comes Helena.

Enter HELENA.

HERMIA	God speed, fair Helena: whither away?	180
HELENA	Call you me fair? That 'fair' again unsay.	
	Demetrius loves your fair: O happy fair!	
	Your eyes are lode-stars, and your tongue's sweet air	
	More tunable than lark to shepherd's ear	
	When wheat is green, when hawthorn buds appear.	
	Sickness is catching: O, were favour so!	
	Your words I catch,[13] fair Hermia; ere I go,	
	My ear should catch your voice, my eye your eye;	
	My tongue should catch your tongue's sweet melody.	
	Were the world mine, Demetrius being bated,	190
	The rest I'd give to be to you translated.	
	O, teach me how you look, and with what art	
	You sway the motion of Demetrius' heart.	
HERMIA	I frown upon him; yet he loves me still.	
HELENA	O that your frowns would teach my smiles such skill!	
HERMIA	I give him curses; yet he gives me love.	
HELENA	O that my prayers could such affection move!	
HERMIA	The more I hate, the more he follows me.	
HELENA	The more I love, the more he hateth me.	
HERMIA	His folly, Helen, is no fault of mine.	200
HELENA	None but your beauty; would that fault were mine!	
HERMIA	Take comfort: he no more shall see my face:	
	Lysander and myself will fly this place.	
	Before the time I did Lysander see,	
	Seemed Athens as a paradise to me:	
	O then, what graces in my love do dwell,	
	That he hath turned a heaven unto a hell!	
LYSANDER	Helen, to you our minds we will unfold:	
	Tomorrow night, when Phoebe doth behold	
	Her silver visage in the wat'ry glass,	210
	Decking with liquid pearl the bladed grass –	
	A time that lovers' flights doth still conceal –	
	Through Athens' gates have we devised to steal.	
HERMIA	And in the wood, where often you and I	
	Upon faint primrose beds were wont to lie,	
	Emptying our bosoms of their counsel sweet,	
	There my Lysander and myself shall meet,	

    And thence from Athens turn away our eyes,
    To seek new friends and stranger companies.
    Farewell, sweet playfellow: pray thou for us;   220
    And good luck grant thee thy Demetrius!
    Keep word, Lysander: we must starve our sight
    From lovers' food till morrow deep midnight.

LYSANDER I will, my Hermia. [*Exit Hermia.*] Helena, adieu:
    As you on him, Demetrius dote on you!

                           [*Exit Lysander.*

HELENA   How happy some o'er other some can be![14]
    Through Athens I am thought as fair as she,
    But what of that? Demetrius thinks not so:
    He will not know what all but he do know.
    And as he errs, doting on Hermia's eyes,   230
    So I, admiring of his qualities.
    Things base and vile, holding no quantity,[15]
    Love can transpose to form and dignity.
    Love looks not with the eyes, but with the mind:
    And therefore is winged Cupid painted blind.
    Nor hath Love's mind of any judgment taste:
    Wings and no eyes figure unheedy haste.
    And therefore is Love said to be a child,
    Because in choice he is so oft beguiled.
    As waggish boys in game themselves forswear,   240
    So the boy Love is perjured every where.
    For, ere Demetrius looked on Hermia's eyne,
    He hailed down oaths that he was only mine.
    And when this hail some heat from Hermia felt,
    So he dissolved, and show'rs of oaths did melt.
    I will go tell him of fair Hermia's flight:
    Then to the wood will he tomorrow night
    Pursue her; and for this intelligence,
    If I have thanks, it is a dear expense:[16]
    But herein mean I to enrich my pain,   250
    To have his sight thither and back again.

                           [*Exit.*

SCENE 2.

Athens. Peter Quince's abode.

QUINCE, BOTTOM, SNUG, FLUTE, SNOUT *and* STARVELING.[17]

QUINCE   Is all our company here?

BOTTOM   You were best to call them generally, man by man, according to the scrip.

QUINCE   Here is the scroll of every man's name which is thought fit, through all Athens, to play in our interlude before the duke and the duchess, on his wedding-day at night.

BOTTOM   First, good Peter Quince, say what the play treats on: then read the names of the actors: and so grow to a point.

QUINCE   Marry, our play is 'The Most Lamentable Comedy,   10 and Most Cruel Death, of Pyramus and Thisby'.[18]

BOTTOM   A very good piece of work, I assure you, and a merry. Now, good Peter Quince, call forth your actors by the scroll. Masters, spread yourselves.

QUINCE   Answer, as I call you. Nick Bottom, the weaver?

BOTTOM   Ready: name what part I am for, and proceed.

QUINCE   You, Nick Bottom, are set down for Pyramus.

BOTTOM   What is Pyramus? A lover, or a tyrant?

QUINCE   A lover that kills himself, most gallant, for love.

BOTTOM   That will ask some tears in the true performing of it. If   20 I do it, let the audience look to their eyes: I will move storms: I will condole, in some measure. To the rest — yet my chief humour is for a tyrant. I could play Ercles rarely, or a part to tear a cat in, to make all split.

       'The raging rocks
        And shivering shocks
        Shall break the locks
          Of prison-gates;
        And Phibbus' car
        Shall shine from far,   30
        And make and mar
          The foolish Fates.'[19]

This was lofty. Now, name the rest of the players. — This is Ercles' vein, a tyrant's vein; a lover is more condoling.

QUINCE   Francis Flute, the bellows-mender?

FLUTE   Here, Peter Quince.

QUINCE   Flute, you must take Thisby on you.

FLUTE   What is Thisby? A wand'ring knight?

QUINCE   It is the lady that Pyramus must love.

FLUTE   Nay, faith: let not me play a woman: I have a beard 40
           coming.

QUINCE   That's all one: you shall play it in a mask; and you may
           speak as small as you will.

BOTTOM   An I may hide my face, let me play Thisby too: I'll
           speak in a monstrous little voice. 'Thisny? Thisny?'[20] –
           'Ah, Pyramus, my lover dear, thy Thisby dear, and
           lady dear.'

QUINCE   No, no, you must play Pyramus; and Flute, you
           Thisby.

BOTTOM   Well, proceed.   50

QUINCE   Robin Starveling, the tailor?

STARV'LING Here, Peter Quince.

QUINCE   Robin Starveling, you must play Thisby's mother. Tom
           Snout, the tinker?

SNOUT   Here, Peter Quince.

QUINCE   You, Pyramus' father; myself, Thisby's father; Snug,
           the joiner, you the lion's part: and I hope here is a play
           fitted.

SNUG   Have you the lion's part written? Pray you, if it be,
           give it me: for I am slow of study.   60

QUINCE   You may do it extempore, for it is nothing but roaring.

BOTTOM   Let me play the lion too. I will roar, that I will do any
           man's heart good to hear me. I will roar, that I will make
           the duke say: 'Let him roar again – let him roar again!'

QUINCE   An you should do it too terribly, you would fright the
           duchess and the ladies, that they would shriek: and that
           were enough to hang us all.

ALL   That would hang us, every mother's son.

BOTTOM   I grant you, friends, if you should fright the ladies out
           of their wits, they would have no more discretion but 70
           to hang us; but I will aggravate my voice so, that I will
           roar you as gently as any sucking dove: I will roar you
           an 'twere any nightingale.

QUINCE   You can play no part but Pyramus: for Pyramus is a
           sweet-faced man; a proper man as one shall see in a
           summer's day; a most lovely, gentleman-like man:
           therefore you must needs play Pyramus.

BOTTOM   Well, I will undertake it. What beard were I best to
           play it in?

QUINCE   Why, what you will.   80

BOTTOM   I will discharge it in either your straw-colour beard,
           your orange-tawny beard, your purple-in-grain beard,
           or your French-crown-colour beard, your perfect
           yellow.

QUINCE   Some of your French crowns have no hair at all; and
           then you will play barefaced.[21] [*He distributes strips of
           paper among them:*] But, masters, here are your parts, and
           I am to entreat you, request you, and desire you, to con
           them by tomorrow night; and meet me in the palace
           wood, a mile without the town, by moonlight. There   90
           will we rehearse: for if we meet in the city, we shall be
           dogged with company, and our devices known. In the
           meantime, I will draw a bill of properties such as our
           play wants. I pray you fail me not.

BOTTOM   We will meet, and there we may rehease most obscenely
           and courageously. Take pains, be perfect; adieu.

QUINCE   At the duke's oak we meet.

BOTTOM   Enough: hold, or cut bow-strings.[22]

                                                          [*Exeunt.*

ACT 2, SCENE 1.

Night. The palace wood.

Enter, separately, ROBIN GOODFELLOW *and a* FAIRY.[23]

ROBIN   How now, spirit! Whither wander you?
FAIRY   Over hill, over dale,
        Thorough bush, thorough briar,
      Over park, over pale,
        Thorough flood, thorough fire:
      I do wander everywhere,
      Swifter than the moon's sphere;[24]
      And I serve the Fairy Queen,
      To dew her orbs upon the green.[25]
      The cowslips tall her pensioners be;   10
      In their gold coats spots you see:
      Those be rubies, fairy favours:
      In those freckles live their savours.
  I must go seek some dewdrops here,
  And hang a pearl in every cowslip's ear.
  Farewell, thou lob of spirits; I'll be gone.
  Our queen and all her elves come here anon.
ROBIN   The king doth keep his revels here tonight.
  Take heed the queen come not within his sight,
  For Oberon is passing fell and wrath   20
  Because that she as her attendant hath
  A lovely boy, stol'n from an Indian king:
  She never had so sweet a changeling.[26]
  And jealous Oberon would have the child
  Knight of his train, to trace the forests wild.
  But she, perforce, withholds the lovèd boy,
  Crowns him with flowers, and makes him all her joy.
  And now they never meet in grove, or green,
  By fountain clear, or spangled starlight sheen,
  But they do square — that all their elves, for fear,   30
  Creep into acorn cups, and hide them there.
FAIRY   Either I mistake your shape and making quite,
  Or else you are that shrewd and knavish sprite

Called Robin Goodfellow. Are not you he
That frights the maidens of the villagery,
Skim milk, and sometimes labour in the quern,
And bootless make the breathless housewife churn,
And sometime make the drink to bear no barm,
Mislead night-wanderers, laughing at their harm?
Those that 'Hobgoblin' call you, and 'sweet Puck',   40
You do their work, and they shall have good luck.
Are not you he?

ROBIN   Thou speak'st aright;
I am that merry wanderer of the night.
I jest to Oberon, and make him smile
When I a fat and bean-fed horse beguile,
Neighing in likeness of a filly foal;
And sometime lurk I in a gossip's bowl,
In very likeness of a roasted crab,[27]
And, when she drinks, against her lips I bob,
And on her withered dewlap pour the ale.   50
The wisest aunt, telling the saddest tale,
Sometime for three-foot stool mistaketh me:
Then slip I from her bum, down topples she,
And 'Tailor!' cries,[28] and falls into a cough;
And then the whole choir hold their hips and laugh,
And waxen in their mirth, and neeze, and swear
A merrier hour was never wasted there.
But room, fairy: here comes Oberon.[29]

FAIRY   And here my mistress. Would that he were gone.

Enter from one side, OBERON *and his* RETINUE, *and,
from the other side,* TITANIA *and her* RETINUE.[30]

OBERON   Ill met by moonlight, proud Titania.   60
TITANIA   What, jealous Oberon! Fairies, skip hence –
I have forsworn his bed and company.
OBERON   Tarry, rash wanton. Am not I thy lord?
TITANIA   Then I must be thy lady; but I know
When thou hast stol'n away from fairy land,
And in the shape of Corin sat all day,
Playing on pipes of corn, and versing love
To amorous Phillida.[31] Why art thou here,
Come from the farthest steep of India?

But that, forsooth, the bouncing Amazon,   70
Your buskined mistress and your warrior love,
To Theseus must be wedded; and you come
To give their bed joy and prosperity.

OBERON How canst thou thus, for shame, Titania,
Glance at my credit with Hippolyta,
Knowing I know thy love to Theseus?
Didst thou not lead him through the glimmering night
From Perigouna, whom he ravishèd,
And make him with fair Aegles break his faith,
With Ariadne, and Antiopa?[32]   80

TITANIA These are the forgeries of jealousy;
And never, since the middle summer's spring,
Met we on hill, in dale, forest, or mead,
By pavèd fountain, or by rushy brook,
Or in the beachèd margent of the sea,
To dance our ringlets to the whistling wind,
But with thy brawls thou hast disturbed our sport.
Therefore the winds, piping to us in vain,
As in revenge have sucked up from the sea
Contagious fogs: which, falling in the land,   90
Hath every pelting river made so proud
That they have overborne their continents.
The ox hath therefore stretched his yoke in vain,
The ploughman lost his sweat, and the green corn
Hath rotted ere his youth attained a beard;
The fold stands empty in the drownèd field,
And crows are fatted with the murrion flock;
The nine men's morris[33] is filled up with mud,
And the quaint mazes in the wanton green[34]
For lack of tread are undistinguishable.   100
The human mortals want their winter cheer;[35]
No night is now with hymn or carol blest;
Therefore the moon (the governess of floods),
Pale in her anger, washes all the air,
That rheúmatic diseases do abound.
And, thórough this distemperature, we see
The seasons alter: hoary-headed frosts
Fall in the fresh lap of the crimson rose,

And on old Hiems' thin and icy crown[36]
An odorous chaplet of sweet summer buds   110
Is, as in mockery, set. The spring, the summer,
The childing autumn, angry winter, change
Their wonted liveries; and the mazèd world,
By their increase, now knows not which is which.
And this same progeny of evils comes
From our debate, from our dissension:
We are their parents and original.

OBERON   Do you amend it then: it lies in you.
Why should Titania cross her Oberon?
I do but beg a little changeling boy,   120
To be my henchman.

TITANIA   Set your heart at rest.
The fairy land buys not the child of me.
His mother was a vot'ress of my order;
And in the spicèd Indian air, by night,
Full often hath she gossiped by my side;
And sat with me on Neptune's yellow sands,
Marking th'embarkèd traders on the flood;
When we have laughed to see the sails conceive
And grow big-bellied with the wanton wind;
Which she, with pretty and with swimming gait   130
Following (her womb then rich with my young squire),
Would imitate, and sail upon the land,
To fetch me trifles, and return again,
As from a voyage, rich with merchandise.
But she, being mortal, of that boy did die;
And for her sake do I rear up her boy;
And for her sake I will not part with him.

OBERON   How long within this wood intend you stay?

TITANIA   Perchance till after Theseus' wedding-day.
If you will patiently dance in our round,   140
And see our moonlight revels, go with us;
If not, shun me, and I will spare your haunts.

OBERON   Give me that boy, and I will go with thee.

TITANIA   Not for thy fairy kingdom. Fairies, away!
We shall chide downright, if I longer stay.

                         [*Exeunt Titania and her retinue.*

OBERON   Well, go thy way. Thou shalt not from this grove
           Till I torment thee for this injury.
           My gentle Puck, come hither. Thou rememb'rest
           Since once I sat upon a promontory,
           And heard a mermaid, on a dolphin's back,   150
           Uttering such dulcet and harmonious breath
           That the rude sea grew civil at her song,
           And certain stars shot madly from their spheres
           To hear the sea-maid's music.[37]
ROBIN   I remember.
OBERON   That very time I saw (but thou couldst not),
           Flying between the cold moon and the earth,
           Cupid, all armed: a certain aim he took
           At a fair vestal, thronèd by the west,
           And loosed his love-shaft smartly from his bow,
           As it should pierce a hundred thousand hearts;   160
           But I might see young Cupid's fiery shaft
           Quenched in the chaste beams of the wat'ry moon:
           And the imperial vot'ress passèd on,
           In maiden meditation, fancy-free.[38]
           Yet marked I where the bolt of Cupid fell.
           It fell upon a little western flower;
           Before, milk-white; now purple with love's wound:
           And maidens call it 'Love-in-Idleness'.[39]
           Fetch me that flower, the herb I showed thee once.
           The juice of it, on sleeping eyelids laid,   170
           Will make or man or woman madly dote
           Upon the next live creature that it sees.
           Fetch me this herb, and be thou here again
           Ere the leviathan can swim a league.
ROBIN   I'll put a girdle round about the earth
           In forty minutes.   [*Exit.*
OBERON   Having once this juice,
           I'll watch Titania when she is asleep,
           And drop the liquor of it in her eyes:
           The next thing then she, waking, looks upon
           (Be it on lion, bear, or wolf, or bull,   180
           On meddling monkey, or on busy ape),
           She shall pursue it with the soul of love.

And ere I take this charm from off her sight
(As I can take it with another herb),
I'll make her render up her page to me.
But who comes here? I am invisible,
And I will overhear their conference.

Enters DEMETRIUS, *followed by* HELENA.

DEMETR. I love thee not: therefore pursue me not.
Where is Lysander and fair Hermia?
The one I'll slay; the other slayeth me.   190
Thou told'st me they were stol'n unto this wood:
And here am I, and wood within this wood,[40]
Because I cannot meet my Hermia:
Hence, get thee gone, and follow me no more.

HELENA You draw me, you hard-hearted adamant;
But yet you draw not iron, for my heart
Is true as steel. Leave you your power to draw,
And I shall have no power to follow you.[41]

DEMETR. Do I entice you? Do I speak you fair?
Or rather do I not in plainest truth   200
Tell you I do not nor I cannot love you?

HELENA And even for that do I love you the more:
I am your spaniel; and, Demetrius,
The more you beat me, I will fawn on you.
Use me but as your spaniel: spurn me, strike me,
Neglect me, lose me; only give me leave
(Unworthy as I am) to follow you.
What worser place can I beg in your love
(And yet, a place of high respect with me)
Than to be usèd as you use your dog?   210

DEMETR. Tempt not too much the hatred of my spirit,
For I am sick when I do look on thee.

HELENA And I am sick when I look not on you.

DEMETR. You do impeach your módesty too much,
To leave the city and commit yourself
Into the hands of one that loves you not,
To trust the opportunity of night
And the ill counsel of a desert place
With the rich worth of your virginity.

HELENA Your virtue is my privilege, for that   220

It is not night when I do see your face:
Therefore I think I am not in the night.
Nor doth this wood lack worlds of company,
For you in my respect are all the world.
Then how can it be said I am alone,
When all the world is here to look on me?

EMETR. I'll run from thee, and hide me in the brakes,
And leave thee to the mercy of wild beasts.

ELENA The wildest hath not such a heart as you.
Run when you will; the story shall be changed: 230
Apollo flies, and Daphne holds the chase;[42]
The dove pursues the griffin; the mild hind
Makes speed to catch the tiger. Bootless speed,
When cowardice pursues and valour flies.

EMETR. I will not stay thy questions. Let me go;
Or, if thou follow me, do not believe
But I shall do thee mischief in the wood.

ELENA Ay, in the temple, in the town, the field,
You do me mischief. Fie, Demetrius!
Your wrongs do set a scandal on my sex.   240
We cannot fight for love, as men may do;
We should be wooed, and were not made to woo.

           [*Exit Demetrius.*

I'll follow thee and make a heaven of hell,
To die upon the hand I love so well.   [*Exit Helena.*

BERON Fare thee well, nymph. Ere he do leave this grove,
Thou shalt fly him, and he shall seek thy love.

      Enter ROBIN.

Hast thou the flower there? Welcome, wanderer.

OBIN Ay, there it is.

BERON   I pray thee, give it me.
I know a bank whereon the wild thyme blows,[43]
Where oxlips and the nodding violet grows,   250
Quite over-canopied with luscious woodbine,
With sweet musk-roses, and with eglantine:
There sleeps Titania sometime of the night,
Lulled in these flowers with dances and delight;
And there the snake throws her enamelled skin,
Weed wide enough to wrap a fairy in.

And, with the juice of this, I'll streak her eyes,
And make her full of hateful fantasies.
Take thou some of it, and seek through this grove.
A sweet Athenian lady is in love   2
With a disdainful youth: anoint his eyes –
But do it when the next thing he espies
May be the lady. Thou shalt know the man
By the Athenian garments he hath on.
Effect it with some care, that he may prove
More fond on her than she upon her love;
And look thou meet me ere the first cock crow.

ROBIN   Fear not, my lord: your servant shall do so.

                                     [*Exeunt.*

SCENE 2.

The wood. Enter TITANIA *with her* RETINUE.

TITANIA   Come now, a roundel and a fairy song;
Then, for the third part of a minute, hence:
Some to kill cankers in the musk-rose buds,
Some war with rere-mice for their leathern wings
To make my small elves coats, and some keep back
The clamorous owl that nightly hoots and wonders
At our quaint spirits. Sing me now asleep;
Then to your offices, and let me rest.

        She reclines. Fairies sing and dance.

FAIRY I   You spotted snakes with double tongue,
      Thorny hedgehogs, be not seen;   I
Newts and blind-worms, do no wrong:
      Come not near our Fairy Queen.

CHORUS   Philomele,[44] with melody,
      Sing in our sweet lullaby;
        Lulla, lulla, lullaby,
        Lulla, lulla, lullaby.
     Never harm,
     Nor spell, nor charm,
   Come our lovely lady nigh.
   So good night, with lullaby.   2

AIRY 1	Weaving spiders, come not here: 　　Hence, you long-legg'd spinners, hence. Beetles black, approach not near; 　　Worm nor snail do no offence.
HORUS	Philomele, with melody, 　　Sing in our sweet lullaby; 　　　　Lulla, lulla, lullaby, 　　　　Lulla, lulla, lullaby. 　　　Never harm, 　　　Nor spell, nor charm,　　　　　　　　30 　　Come our lovely lady nigh. So good night, with lullaby. 　　*[Titania sleeps.*
AIRY 2	Hence, away: now all is well. One aloof stand sentinel.　　　　*[Exeunt fairies.*

Enter OBERON. *He drips the juice upon Titania's eyelids.*

OBERON	What thou see'st when thou dost wake, Do it for thy true-love take: Love and languish for his sake. Be it ounce, or cat, or bear, Pard, or boar with bristled hair, In thy eye that shall appear　　　　　　40 When thou wak'st, it is thy dear: Wake when some vile thing is near. 　　*[Exit.*

Enter LYSANDER *and* HERMIA.

LYSANDER	Fair love, you faint with wand'ring in the wood; 　　And, to speak troth, I have forgot our way. We'll rest us, Hermia, if you think it good, 　　And tarry for the comfort of the day.
HERMIA	Be't so, Lysander: find you out a bed: For I upon this bank will rest my head.
LYSANDER	One turf shall serve as pillow for us both: One heart, one bed, two bosoms, and one troth.　　50
HERMIA	Nay, good Lysander: for my sake, my dear, Lie further off yet; do not lie so near.
LYSANDER	O take the sense, sweet, of my innocence! Love takes the meaning in love's conference.[45] I mean that my heart unto yours is knit, So that but one heart we can make of it:

Two bosoms interchainèd with an oath:
So then two bosoms and a single troth.
Then by your side no bed-room me deny,
For lying so, Hermia, I do not lie.   6

HERMIA   Lysander riddles very prettily.
Now much beshrew my manners and my pride,
If Hermia meant to say Lysander lied.
But, gentle friend, for love and courtesy
Lie further off, in human modesty:
Such separation as may well be said
Becomes a virtuous bachelor and a maid.
So far be distant; and good night, sweet friend:
Thy love ne'er alter till thy sweet life end!

LYSANDER   Amen, amen, to that fair prayer, say I;   7
And then end life when I end loyalty!
Here is my bed: sleep give thee all his rest.

HERMIA   With half that wish, the wisher's eyes be pressed.

                                [They sleep.

Enter ROBIN.

ROBIN   Through the forest have I gone,
But Athenian found I none
On whose eyes I might approve
This flower's force in stirring love.
Night and silence. – Who is here?
Weeds of Athens he doth wear:
This is he, my master said,   8
Despisèd the Athenian maid;
And here the maiden, sleeping sound,
On the dank and dirty ground.
Pretty soul, she durst not lie
Near this lack-love, this kill-courtesy.[46]
Churl, upon thy eyes I throw
All the power this charm doth owe.
              [He drips the juice upon Lysander's eyelids.
When thou wak'st, let love forbid
Sleep his seat on thy eyelid.
So awake when I am gone;   9
For I must now to Oberon.   *[Exit.*

Enter DEMETRIUS *and* HELENA.

HELENA   Stay, though thou kill me, sweet Demetrius.
DEMETR.   I charge thee, hence, and do not haunt me thus.
HELENA   O, wilt thou darkling leave me? Do not so.
DEMETR.   Stay, on thy peril; I alone will go.

                                                              [*Exit.*

HELENA   O, I am out of breath in this fond chase!
           The more my prayer, the lesser is my grace.
           Happy is Hermia, wheresoe'er she lies,
           For she hath blessèd and attractive eyes.
           How came her eyes so bright? Not with salt tears: 100
           If so, my eyes are oft'ner washed than hers.
           No, no: I am as ugly as a bear,
           For beasts that meet me run away for fear.
           Therefore no marvel though Demetrius
           Do, as a monster, fly my presence thus.
           What wicked and dissembling glass of mine
           Made me compare with Hermia's sphery eyne?
           But, who is here? Lysander, on the ground?
           Dead, or asleep? I see no blood, no wound.
           Lysander, if you live, good sir, awake.   110
LYSANDER   [*leaping up:*]
           And run through fire I will, for thy sweet sake!
           Transparent Helena! Nature shows art,
           That through thy bosom makes me see thy heart.
           Where is Demetrius? O, how fit a word
           Is that vile name to perish on my sword!
HELENA   Do not say so, Lysander, say not so.
           What though he love your Hermia? Lord, what
                                                      though?
           Yet Hermia still loves you: then be content.
LYSANDER   Content with Hermia? No: I do repent
           The tedious minutes I with her have spent.   120
           Not Hermia, but Helena I love:
           Who will not change a raven for a dove?
           The will of man is by his reason swayed;
           And reason says you are the worthier maid.
           Things growing are not ripe until their season:
           So I, being young, till now ripe not to reason;

And touching now the point of human skill,
Reason becomes the marshal to my will,
And leads me to your eyes; where I o'erlook
Love's stories, written in love's richest book.   13

HELENA   Wherefore was I to this keen mockery born?
When, at your hands, did I deserve this scorn?
Is't not enough, is't not enough, young man,
That I did never – no, nor never can –
Deserve a sweet look from Demetrius' eye,
But you must flout my insufficiency?
Good troth, you do me wrong (good sooth, you do),
In such disdainful manner me to woo.
But, fare you well: perforce, I must confess,
I thought you lord of more true gentleness.   14
O, that a lady, of one man refused,
Should of another therefore be abused!   [*Exit.*

LYSANDER She sees not Hermia. Hermia, sleep thou there,
And never mayst thou come Lysander near.
For, as a surfeit of the sweetest things
The deepest loathing to the stomach brings,
Or as the heresies that men do leave
Are hated most of those they did deceive,
So thou, my surfeit and my heresy,
Of all be hated, but the most of me;   15
And all my powers, address your love and might
To honour Helen, and to be her knight.   [*Exit.*

HERMIA   [*awaking:*] Help me, Lysander, help me! Do thy best
To pluck this crawling serpent from my breast.
Ay me, for pity. What a dream was here!
Lysander, look how I do quake with fear.
Methought a serpent ate my heart away,
And you sat smiling at his cruel prey.
Lysander – what, removed? Lysander, lord!
What, out of hearing gone? No sound, no word?   16
Alack, where are you? Speak, an if you hear;
Speak, of all loves: I swoon almost with fear.
No? Then I well perceive you are not nigh.
Either death or you I'll find immediately.
                                        [*Exit.*

ACT 3, SCENE I.

The wood.

Enter QUINCE, SNUG, BOTTOM, FLUTE, SNOUT
and STARVELING. *Unseen by them,* TITANIA *sleeps*.

BOTTOM   Are we all met?

QUINCE   Pat, pat; and here's a marvellous convenient place for
our rehearsal. This green plot shall be our stage, this
hawthorn-brake our tiring-house; and we will do it in
action, as we will do it before the duke.

BOTTOM   Peter Quince!

QUINCE   What say'st thou, bully Bottom?

BOTTOM   There are things in this comedy of Pyramus and Thisby
that will never please. First, Pyramus must draw a
sword to kill himself; which the ladies cannot abide.   10
How answer you that?

SNOUT   Berlakin, a parlous fear.

STARV.   I believe we must leave the killing out, when all is
done.

BOTTOM   Not a whit: I have a device to make all well. Write me
a prologue, and let the prologue seem to say we will
do no harm with our swords, and that Pyramus is not
killed indeed; and, for the more better assurance, tell
them that I, Pyramus, am not Pyramus but Bottom the
weaver: this will put them out of fear.   20

QUINCE   Well, we will have such a prologue, and it shall be
written in eight and six.

BOTTOM   No, make it two more: let it be written in eight and
eight.[47]

SNOUT   Will not the ladies be afeard of the lion?

STARV.   I fear it, I promise you.

BOTTOM   Masters, you ought to consider with yourself: to bring
in (God shield us!) a lion among ladies is a most dreadful
thing. For there is not a more fearful wild-fowl than
your lion living; and we ought to look to't.   30

SNOUT   Therefore, another prologue must tell he is not a lion.

BOTTOM   Nay, you must name his name, and half his face must be

seen through the lion's neck, and he himself must speak
through, saying thus, or to the same defect: 'Ladies', or
'Fair ladies — I would wish you', or 'I would request
you', or 'I would entreat you, not to fear, not to trem-
ble: my life for yours. If you think I come hither as a
lion, it were pity of my life. No: I am no such thing: I
am a man as other men are.' And there indeed let him
name his name, and tell them plainly he is Snug the   40
joiner.

QUINCE Well, it shall be so; but there is two hard things: that is,
to bring the moonlight into a chamber: for you know,
Pyramus and Thisby meet by moonlight.

SNOUT Doth the moon shine that night we play our play?

BOTTOM A calendar, a calendar! Look in the almanac: find out
moonshine, find out moonshine.

                    QUINCE *consults an almanac.*

QUINCE Yes, it doth shine that night.

BOTTOM Why, then may you leave a casement of the great
chamber window (where we play) open; and the moon   50
may shine in at the casement.

QUINCE Ay, or else one must come in with a bush of thorns and
a lantern, and say he comes to disfigure or to present
the person of Moonshine. Then, there is another thing:
we must have a wall in the great chamber; for Pyramus
and Thisby (says the story) did talk through the chink
of a wall.

SNOUT You can never bring in a wall. What say you, Bottom?

BOTTOM Some man or other must present Wall; and let him have
some plaster, or some loam, or some rough-cast about   60
him, to signify 'Wall'; and let him hold his fingers
thus,[48] and through that cranny shall Pyramus and
Thisby whisper.

QUINCE If that may be, then all is well. Come, sit down, every
mother's son, and rehearse your parts. Pyramus, you
begin: when you have spoken your speech, enter into
that brake — and so every one according to his cue.

                    Enter ROBIN.

ROBIN What hempen home-spuns have we swagg'ring here,

So near the cradle of the Fairy Queen?
What, a play tóward? I'll be an auditor –   70
An actor too perhaps, if I see cause.

QUINCE   Speak, Pyramus. Thisby, stand forth.

BOTTOM   'Thisby, the flowers have odious savours sweet' –

QUINCE   Odours: 'odorous'.

BOTTOM   – 'odours savours sweet,
  So hath thy breath, my dearest Thisby dear.
But hark, a voice! Stay thou but here a while,
  And by and by I will to thee appear.'   [*Exit.*

ROBIN   [*aside:*] A stranger Pyramus than e'er played here!
                                              [*He follows Bottom.*

FLUTE   Must I speak now?   80

QUINCE   Ay, marry, must you. For you must understand, he
goes but to see a noise that he heard, and is to come
again.

FLUTE   'Most radiant Pyramus, most lily-white of hue,
  Of colour like the red rose on triumphant briar,
Most brisky juvenal, and eke most lovely Jew,[49]
  As true as truest horse that yet would never tire,
I'll meet thee, Pyramus, at Ninny's tomb.'

QUINCE   '*Ninus*' tomb', man![50] Why, you must not speak that
yet! That you answer to Pyramus. You speak all your   90
part at once, cues and all. Pyramus, enter; your cue is
past; it is, 'never tire'.

FLUTE   O – 'As true as truest horse that yet would never tire.'

Enter BOTTOM, *now ass-headed,*[51] *followed by* ROBIN.

BOTTOM   'If I were fair, Thisby, I were only thine.'[52]

QUINCE   O monstrous! O strange! We are haunted.
Pray, masters – fly, masters – help!
                                        [*Exeunt all except Bottom and Robin.*

ROBIN   I'll follow you: I'll lead you about a round,
  Through bog, through bush, through brake, through
                                              briar;
Sometime a horse I'll be, sometime a hound,
  A hog, a headless bear, sometime a fire,   100
And neigh, and bark, and grunt, and roar, and burn,
  Like horse, hound, hog, bear, fire, at every turn.
                                              [*Exit.*

BOTTOM   Why do they run away? This is a knavery of them to
         make me afeard.

Enter SNOUT.

SNOUT   O Bottom, thou art changed! What do I see on thee?

BOTTOM   What do you see? You see an ass-head of your own, do
         you?   [*Exit Snout.*

Enter QUINCE.

QUINCE   Bless thee, Bottom, bless thee! Thou art translated.
                                                         [*Exit.*

BOTTOM   I see their knavery. This is to make an ass of me, to
         fright me, if they could; but I will not stir from this   110
         place, do what they can. I will walk up and down here;
         and I will sing, that they shall hear I am not afraid.
         [*He sings:*]
              The woosel cock, so black of hue,
                 With orange-tawny bill;
              The throstle with his note so true,
                 The wren, with little quill –

TITANIA [*awaking:*]
         What angel wakes me from my flow'ry bed?

BOTTOM   The finch, the sparrow, and the lark,
                    The plain-song cuckoo gray,
                 Whose note full many a man doth mark,   120
                    And dares not answer 'nay' – 53
         For indeed, who would set his wit to so foolish a bird?
         Who would give a bird the lie, though he cry 'cuckoo'
         never so?

TITANIA I pray thee, gentle mortal, sing again.
         Mine ear is much enamoured of thy note;
         So is mine eye enthrallèd to thy shape,
         And thy fair virtue's force (perforce) doth move me,
         On the first view, to say, to swear, I love thee.

BOTTOM   Methinks, mistress, you should have little reason for   130
         that. And yet, to say the truth, reason and love keep
         little company together, nowadays. The more the pity,
         that some honest neighbours will not make them
         friends. Nay, I can gleek upon occasion.

TITANIA Thou art as wise as thou art beautiful.

BOTTOM	Not so, neither: but if I had wit enough to get out of this wood, I have enough to serve mine own turn.
TITANIA	Out of this wood do not desire to go:
	Thou shalt remain here, whether thou wilt or no.
	I am a spirit of no common rate: 140
	The summer still doth tend upon my state;
	And I do love thee: therefore go with me.
	I'll give thee fairies to attend on thee:
	And they shall fetch thee jewels from the deep,
	And sing, while thou on pressèd flowers dost sleep;
	And I will purge thy mortal grossness so,
	That thou shalt like an airy spirit go.[54]
	Peaseblossom, Cobweb, Moth,[55] and Mustardseed!

Enter four fairies: PEASEBLOSSOM, COBWEB,
MOTH *and* MUSTARDSEED.

PEASE.	Ready!
COBWEB	And I –
MOTH	And I –
MUSTARD.	And I –
ALL FOUR	Where shall we go?[56]
TITANIA	Be kind and courteous to this gentleman: 150
	Hop in his walks, and gambol in his eyes,
	Feed him with apricocks and dewberries,
	With purple grapes, green figs, and mulberries;
	The honey-bags steal from the humble-bees,
	And for night-tapers crop their waxen thighs,
	And light them at the fiery glow-worm's eyes,
	To have my love to bed and to arise;
	And pluck the wings from painted butterflies,
	To fan the moonbeams from his sleeping eyes.
	Nod to him, elves, and do him courtesies. 160
PEASE.	Hail, mortal!
COBWEB	Hail!
MOTH	Hail!
MUSTARD.	Hail![57]
BOTTOM	I cry your worships mercy, heartily.[58] I beseech your worship's name.
COBWEB	[*bows.*] Cobweb.
BOTTOM	I shall desire you of more acquaintance, good Master

	Cobweb: if I cut my finger, I shall make bold with
	you. – Your name, honest gentleman? 170
PEASE.	[*bows.*] Peaseblossom.
BOTTOM	I pray you, commend me to Mistress Squash, your
	mother, and to Master Peascod,[59] your father. Good
	Master Peaseblossom, I shall desire you of more ac-
	quaintance too. – Your name, I beseech you sir?
MUSTARD.	[*bows.*] Mustardseed.
BOTTOM	Good Master Mustardseed, I know your patience well.
	That same cowardly, giant-like, Oxbeef hath devoured
	many a gentleman of your house. I promise you, your
	kindred hath made my eyes water ere now. I desire 180
	you of more acquaintance, good Master Mustardseed.
TITANIA	Come, wait upon him; lead him to my bower.
	The moon, methinks, looks with a wat'ry eye;
	And when she weeps, weeps every little flower,
	Lamenting some enforcèd chastity.[60]
	Tie up my love's tongue: bring him silently.

[*Exeunt.*

SCENE 2.

The wood.

Enter OBERON.

OBERON	I wonder if Titania be awaked;
	Then, what it was that next came in her eye,
	Which she must dote on in extremity.

Enter ROBIN.

	Here comes my messenger. How now, mad spirit?
	What night–rule now about this haunted grove?
ROBIN	My mistress with a monster is in love.
	Near to her close and consecrated bower,
	While she was in her dull and sleeping hour,
	A crew of patches, rude mechanicals[61]
	That work for bread upon Athenian stalls, 10
	Were met together to rehearse a play
	Intended for great Theseus' nuptial–day.

The shallowest thick-skin of that barren sort,
Who Pyramus presented in their sport,
Forsook his scene and entered in a brake;
When I did him at this advantage take:
An ass's noll I fixèd on his head.
Anon his Thisby must be answerèd,
And forth my mimic comes. When they him spy —
As wild geese that the creeping fowler eye,   20
Or russet-pated choughs, many in sort,
Rising and cawing at the gun's report,
Sever themselves and madly sweep the sky —
So, at his sight, away his fellows fly;
And at one stamp[62] here o'er and o'er one falls:
He 'Murther!' cries, and help from Athens calls.
Their sense thus weak, lost with their fears thus strong,
Made-senseless things[63] begin to do them wrong:
For briars and thorns at their apparel snatch;
Some sleeves, some hats; from yielders all things catch.   30
I led them on in this distracted fear,
And left sweet Pyramus translated there;
When in that moment (so it came to pass)
Titania waked, and straightway loved an ass.

OBERON   This falls out better than I could devise.
But hast thou yet latched the Athenian's eyes
With the love-juice, as I did bid thee do?

ROBIN   I took him sleeping — that is finished too —
And the Athenian woman by his side;
That, when he waked, of force she must be eyed.   40

Enter DEMETRIUS *and* HERMIA.

OBERON   Stand close; this is the same Athenian.
ROBIN   This is the woman, but not this the man.
DEMETR.   O, why rebuke you him that loves you so?
Lay breath so bitter on your bitter foe.[64]

HERMIA   Now I but chide; but I should use thee worse,
For thou (I fear) hast given me cause to curse.
If thou hast slain Lysander in his sleep,
Being o'er-shoes in blood, plunge in the deep,
And kill me too.

  The sun was not so true unto the day   50
  As he to me. Would he have stol'n away
  From sleeping Hermia? I'll believe as soon,
  This whole earth may be bored, and that the moon
  May through the centre creep and so displease
  Her brother's noontide with th'Antipodes.
  It cannot be but thou hast murthered him —
  So should a murtherer look; so dead, so grim.

DEMETR. So should the murthered look, and so should I,
  Pierced through the heart with your stern cruelty.
  Yet you, the murtherer, look as bright, as clear, 60
  As yonder Venus in her glimmering sphere.[65]

HERMIA What's this to my Lysander? Where is he?
  Ah, good Demetrius, wilt thou give him me?

DEMETR. I had rather give his carcase to my hounds.

HERMIA Out, dog! Out, cur! Thou driv'st me past the bounds
  Of maidens' patience. Hast thou slain him then?
  Henceforth be never numbered among men!
  O, once tell true: tell true, even for my sake:
  Durst thou have looked upon him being awake?
  And hast thou killed him sleeping? O brave touch! 70
  Could not a worm, an adder, do so much?
  An adder did it: for with doubler tongue
  Than thine, thou serpent, never adder stung.

DEMETR. You spend your passion on a misprised mood:
  I am not guilty of Lysander's blood;
  Nor is he dead, for aught that I can tell.

HERMIA I pray thee, tell me then that he is well.

DEMETR. And if I could, what should I get therefore?

HERMIA A privilege never to see me more;
  And from thy hated presence part I so.[66] 80
  See me no more, whether he be dead or no.

                [*Exit.*

DEMETR. There is no following her in this fierce vein.
  Here therefore, for a while, I will remain.
  So sorrow's heaviness doth heavier grow
  For debt that bankrout sleep doth sorrow owe;
  Which now in some slight measure it will pay,
  If for his tender here I make some stay. [*He lies down.*

OBERON   [*to Robin:*] What hast thou done? Thou hast mistaken
                                               quite,
        And laid the love-juice on some true-love's sight.
        Of thy misprision must perforce ensue   90
        Some true love turned, and not a false turned true.
ROBIN   Then fate o'er-rules, that, one man holding troth,
        A million fail, confounding oath on oath.[67]
OBERON   About the wood go swifter than the wind,
        And Helena of Athens look thou find.[68]
        All fancy-sick she is, and pale of cheer
        With sighs of love that costs the fresh blood dear.[69]
        By some illusion see thou bring her here:
        I'll charm his eyes against she do appear.
ROBIN   I go, I go – look how I go –   100
        Swifter than arrow from the Tartar's bow.   [*Exit.*

  OBERON *drips the juice upon the eyelids of the sleeping* DEMETRIUS.

OBERON   Flower of this purple dye,
          Hit with Cupid's archery,
        Sink in apple of his eye.
        When his love he doth espy,
          Let her shine as gloriously
        As the Venus of the sky.
        When thou wak'st, if she be by,
          Beg of her for remedy.

               Enter ROBIN.

ROBIN   Captain of our fairy band,   110
        Helena is here at hand,
        And the youth, mistook by me,
        Pleading for a lover's fee.
        Shall we their fond pageant see?
        Lord, what fools these mortals be!
OBERON   Stand aside. The noise they make
        Will cause Demetrius to awake.
ROBIN   Then will two at once woo one:
        That must needs be sport alone.
        And those things do best please me   120
        That befall prepost'rously.   [*They stand aside.*

Enter HELENA, *followed by* LYSANDER.

LYSANDER Why should you think that I should woo in scorn?
          Scorn and derision never come in tears.
        Look when I vow, I weep; and vows so born,
          In their nativity all truth appears.
        How can these things in me seem scorn to you,
        Bearing the badge of faith to prove them true?

HELENA   You do advance your cunning more and more.
          When truth kills truth, O devilish-holy fray!
        These vows are Hermia's − will you give her o'er?   130
          Weigh oath with oath, and you will nothing weigh:
        Your vows, to her and me, put in two scales,
        Will even weigh; and both as light as tales.

LYSANDER I had no judgement when to her I swore.

HELENA   Nor none, in my mind, now you give her o'er.

LYSANDER Demetrius loves her, and he loves not you.

DEMETR. [*awaking:*] O Helen, goddess, nymph, perfect, divine!
        To what, my love, shall I compare thine eyne?
        Crystal is muddy. O, how ripe in show
        Thy lips, those kissing cherries, tempting grow!   140
        That pure congealed white, high Taurus' snow[70]
        Fanned with the eastern wind, turns to a crow,
        When thou hold'st up thy hand. O let me kiss
        This princess of pure white, this seal of bliss!

HELENA   O spite! O hell! I see, you all are bent
        To set against me for your merriment.
        If you were civil, and knew courtesy,
        You would not do me thus much injury.
        Can you not hate me, as I know you do,
        But you must join in souls to mock me too?   150
        If you were men, as men you are in show,
        You would not use a gentle lady so:
        To vow, and swear, and superpraise my parts,
        When I am sure you hate me with your hearts.
        You both are rivals, and love Hermia;
        And now both rivals to mock Helena.
        A trim exploit, a manly enterprise,
        To conjure tears up in a poor maid's eyes
        With your derision! None of noble sort

Would so offend a virgin, and extort   160
A poor soul's patience, all to make you sport.

LYSANDER You are unkind, Demetrius; be not so –
For you love Hermia: this you know I know.
And here, with all good will, with all my heart,
In Hermia's love I yield you up my part;
And yours of Helena to me bequeath,
Whom I do love, and will do till my death.

HELENA Never did mockers waste more idle breath.

DEMETR. Lysander, keep thy Hermia: I will none.
If e'er I loved her, all that love is gone.   170
My heart to her but as guest-wise sojourned,
And now to Helen is it home returned,
There to remain.

LYSANDER   Helen, it is not so.

DEMETR. Disparage not the faith thou dost not know,
Lest to thy peril thou aby it dear.

Enter HERMIA.

Look where thy love comes: yonder is thy dear.

HERMIA *hastens to* LYSANDER.

HERMIA Dark night, that from the eye his function takes,
The ear more quick of apprehension makes.
Wherein it doth impair the seeing sense,
It pays the hearing double recompense.   180
Thou art not by mine eye, Lysander, found:
Mine ear, I thank it, brought me to thy sound.
But why, unkindly, didst thou leave me so?

LYSANDER Why should he stay, whom love doth press to go?

HERMIA What love could press Lysander from my side?

LYSANDER Lysander's love, that would not let him bide:
Fair Helena, who more engilds the night
Than all yon fiery oes and eyes of light.[71]
Why seek'st thou me? Could not this make thee know
The hate I bear thee made me leave thee so?   190

HERMIA You speak not as you think: it cannot be.

HELENA Lo! She is one of this confederacy.
Now I perceive they have conjoined all three
To fashion this false sport in spite of me.

Injurious Hermia, most ungrateful maid,
Have you conspired, have you with these contrived,
To bait me with this foul derision?
Is all the counsel that we two have shared,
The sisters' vows, the hours that we have spent,
When we have chid the hasty-footed time   20
For parting us; O, O! Is all forgot?[72]
All school-days' friendship, childhood innocence?
We, Hermia, like two artificial gods,
Have with our needles created both one flower,
Both on one sampler, sitting on one cushion,
Both warbling of one song, both in one key;
As if our hands, our sides, voices, and minds,
Had been incorporate. So we grew together,
Like to a double cherry, seeming parted,
But yet an union in partition,   21
Two lovely berries moulded on one stem:
So, with two seeming bodies, but one heart –
Two of the first, like coats in heraldry,
Due but to one, and crownèd with one crest.[73]
And will you rend our ancient love asunder,
To join with men in scorning your poor friend?
It is not friendly, 'tis not maidenly.
Our sex, as well as I, may chide you for it;
Though I alone do feel the injury.

HERMIA   I am amazèd at your passionate words.[74]   22
           I scorn you not. It seems that you scorn me.

HELENA   Have you not set Lysander, as in scorn,
           To follow me and praise my eyes and face?
           And made your other love, Demetrius
           (Who even but now did spurn me with his foot),
           To call me goddess, nymph, divine, and rare,
           Precious, celestial? Wherefore speaks he this
           To her he hates? And wherefore doth Lysander
           Deny your love (so rich within his soul)
           And tender me (forsooth!) affection,   23
           But by your setting on, by your consent?
           What though I be not so in grace as you,
           So hung upon with love, so fortunate,

	But miserable most, to love unloved?
	This you should pity, rather than despise.
HERMIA	I understand not what you mean by this.
HELENA	Ay, do![75] Perséver, counterfeit sad looks,
	Make mouths upon me when I turn my back,
	Wink at each other, hold the sweet jest up.
	This sport, well carried, shall be chronicled. 240
	If you have any pity, grace, or manners,
	You would not make me such an argument.
	But, fare ye well: 'tis partly my own fault,
	Which death or absence soon shall remedy.
LYSANDER	Stay, gentle Helena; hear my excuse,
	My love, my life, my soul, fair Helena!
HELENA	O excellent!
HERMIA	[to Lysander:] Sweet, do not scorn her so.
DEMETR.	[to Lysander:] If she cannot entreat, I can compel.
LYSANDER	Thou canst compel no more than she entreat.
	Thy threats have no more strength than her weak
	prayers. 250
	Helen, I love thee – by my life I do;
	I swear by that which I will lose for thee,
	To prove him false that says I love thee not.
DEMETR.	[to Helena:] I say I love thee more than he can do.
LYSANDER	[to Demetrius:] If thou say so, withdraw, and
	prove it too.
DEMETR.	Quick, come –
HERMIA	[restraining him:] Lysander, whereto tends all this?
LYSANDER	Away, you Ethiop!
DEMETR.	No, no, sir: you will
	Seem to break loose,[76] take on as you would follow,
	But yet come not. You are a tame man, go!
LYSANDER	[to Hermia:] Hang off, thou cat, thou bur! Vile
	thing, let loose; 260
	Or I will shake thee from me like a serpent.
HERMIA	Why are you grown so rude? What change is this,
	Sweet love?
LYSANDER	Thy love? Out, tawny Tartar, out!
	Out, loath'd med'cine! O hated potion, hence![77]

HERMIA   Do you not jest?

HELENA   [to Hermia:]   Yes, sooth; and so do you.

LYSANDER   Demetrius, I will keep my word with thee.

DEMETR.   I would I had your bond, for I perceive
            A weak bond holds you. I'll not trust your word.

LYSANDER   What? Should I hurt her, strike her, kill her dead?
            Although I hate her, I'll not harm her so.   27

HERMIA   What? Can you do me greater harm than hate?
            Hate me, wherefore? O me, what news, my love!
            Am not I Hermia? Are not you Lysander?
            I am as fair now as I was erewhile.
            Since night you loved me; yet since night you left me.
            Why then, you left me (O, the gods forbid!)
            In earnest, shall I say?

LYSANDER   Ay, by my life;
            And never did desire to see thee more.
            Therefore be out of hope, of question, doubt:[78]
            Be certain: nothing truer: 'tis no jest   28
            That I do hate thee and love Helena.

HERMIA   [to Helena:] O me, you juggler, you canker-blossom.[79]
            You thief of love! What, have you come by night
            And stol'n my love's heart from him?

HELENA   Fine, i'faith!
            Have you no modesty, no maiden shame,
            No touch of bashfulness? What, will you tear
            Impatient answers from my gentle tongue?
            Fie, fie, you counterfeit, you puppet, you![80]

HERMIA   'Puppet'? Why so? Ay, that way goes the game.
            Now I perceive that she hath made compare   29
            Between our statures; she hath urged her height;
            And with her pers'nage, her tall personage,
            Her height (forsooth), she hath prevailed with him.
            And are you grown so high in his esteem
            Because I am so dwarfish and so low?
            How low am I, thou painted maypole? Speak:
            How low am I? I am not yet so low,
            But that my nails can reach unto thine eyes.

HELENA   I pray you, though you mock me, gentlemen,
            Let her not hurt me. I was never curst: 30

I have no gift at all in shrewishness;
I am a right maid for my cowardice:
Let her not strike me. You perhaps may think,
Because she is something lower than myself,
That I can match her.

HERMIA   'Lower'? Hark again.

HELENA   Good Hermia, do not be so bitter with me.
I evermore did love you, Hermia,
Did ever keep your counsels, never wronged you;
Save that, in love unto Demetrius,
I told him of your stealth unto this wood.   310
He followed you; for love, I followed him.
But he hath chid me hence, and threatened me
To strike me, spurn me; nay, to kill me too.
And now, so you will let me quiet go,
To Athens will I bear my folly back,
And follow you no further. Let me go.
You see how simple and how fond I am.

HERMIA   Why, get you gone. Who is't that hinders you?

HELENA   A foolish heart that I leave here behind.

HERMIA   What! With Lysander?

HELENA   With Demetrius.   320

LYSANDER Be not afraid: she shall not harm thee, Helena.

DEMETR.   No, sir; she shall not, though you take her part.

HELENA   O, when she's angry, she is keen and shrewd.
She was a vixen when she went to school;
And though she be but little, she is fierce.

HERMIA   'Little' again? Nothing but 'low' and 'little'?
Why will you suffer her to flout me thus?
Let me come to her.

LYSANDER   Get you gone, you dwarf;
You minimus, of hind'ring knot-grass made;
You bead, you acorn.

DEMETR.   You are too officious   330
In her behalf that scorns your services.
Let her alone; speak not of Helena;
Take not her part; [*He draws his sword.*]
                         for if thou dost intend
Never so little show of love to her,

Thou shalt aby it.

LYSANDER   [*also draws.*]   Now she holds me not;
Now follow, if thou dar'st, to try whose right,
Of thine or mine, is most in Helena.

DEMETR.   'Follow'? Nay, I'll go with thee, cheek by jowl.

                                [*Exeunt Lysander and Demetrius.*

HERMIA   You, mistress, all this coil is 'long of you.
Nay: go not back.

HELENA   I will not trust you, I,   340
Nor longer stay in your curst company.
Your hands than mine are quicker for a fray;
My legs are longer though, to run away.   [*She runs off.*

HERMIA   I am amazed, and know not what to say.

                                          [*Exit.*

OBERON   [*to Robin:*] This is thy negligence. Still thou mistak'st,
Or else commit'st thy knaveries wilfully.

ROBIN   Believe me, king of shadows, I mistook.
Did not you tell me, I should know the man
By the Athenian garments he had on?
And so far blameless proves my enterprise   350
That I have 'nointed an Athenian's eyes;
And so far am I glad, it so did sort,
As this their jangling I esteem a sport.

OBERON   Thou see'st, these lovers seek a place to fight:
Hie therefore, Robin, overcast the night,
The starry welkin cover thou anon
With drooping fog as black as Acheron,
And lead these testy rivals so astray,
As one come not within another's way.
Like to Lysander sometime frame thy tongue;   360
Then stir Demetrius up with bitter wrong;
And sometime rail thou like Demetrius;
And from each other look thou lead them thus,
Till o'er their brows death-counterfeiting sleep
With leaden legs and batty wings doth creep.
Then crush this herb into Lysander's eye;
Whose liquor hath this virtuous property,
To take from thence all error with his might,
And make his eyeballs roll with wonted sight.

When they next wake, all this derision   370
Shall seem a dream and fruitless vision,
And back to Athens shall the lovers wend
With league whose date till death shall never end.
Whiles I in this affair do thee employ,
I'll to my queen and beg her Indian boy;
And then I will her charmèd eye release
From monster's view, and all things shall be peace.

ROBIN   My fairy lord, this must be done with haste,
For night's swift dragons cut the clouds full fast;
And yonder shines Aurora's harbinger,[81]   380
At whose approach, ghosts, wand'ring here and there,
Troop home to churchyards. Damnèd spirits all,
That in crossways and floods have burial,
Already to their wormy beds are gone,
For fear lest day should look their shames upon.
They wilfully themselves exile from light,
And must for aye consort with black-browed night.

OBERON   But we are spirits of another sort.
I, with the morning's love, have oft made sport,
And, like a forester, the groves may tread,   390
Even till the eastern gate all fiery-red,
Opening on Neptune, with fair blessèd beams
Turns into yellow gold his salt green streams.[82]
But notwithstanding, haste, make no delay:
We may effect this business yet ere day.   [*Exit.*

ROBIN   Up and down, up and down,
          I will lead them up and down.
          I am feared in field and town.
          Goblin,[83] lead them up and down.
Here comes one.   400

Enter LYSANDER.

LYSANDER Where art thou, proud Demetrius? Speak thou now.
ROBIN   Here, villain! Drawn and ready. Where art thou?
LYSANDER I will be with thee straight.
ROBIN   Follow me then
          To plainer ground.   [*Exit Lysander.*

Enter DEMETRIUS.

DEMETR.   Lysander, speak again.
          Thou runaway, thou coward, art thou fled?
          Speak! In some bush?[84] Where dost thou hide thy head?

ROBIN   Thou coward, art thou bragging to the stars,
          Telling the bushes that thou look'st for wars,
          And wilt not come? Come, recreant; come, thou child;
          I'll whip thee with a rod. He is defiled   410
          That draws a sword on thee.

DEMETR.   .   Yea, art thou there?

ROBIN   Follow my voice: we'll try no manhood here.

                                        [*Exeunt.*

Enter LYSANDER.

LYSANDER He goes before me, and still dares me on;
          When I come where he calls, then he is gone.
          The villain is much lighter-heeled than I:
          I followed fast; but faster he did fly,
          That fall'n am I in dark uneven way;
          And here will rest me. [*He lies down.*]
                              Come, thou gentle day,
          For if but once thou show me thy grey light,
          I'll find Demetrius, and revenge this spite.   [*He sleeps.* 420

Enter ROBIN *and* DEMETRIUS.

ROBIN   Ho, ho, ho, ho! Coward, why com'st thou not?[85]

DEMETR.   Abide me if thou dar'st, for well I wot
          Thou runn'st before me, shifting every place,
          And dar'st not stand, nor look me in the face.
          Where art thou now?

ROBIN   [*shifting place:*]   Come hither; I am here.

DEMETR.   Nay then thou mock'st me. Thou shalt buy this dear,
          If ever I thy face by daylight see.
          Now, go thy way. Faintness constraineth me
          To measure out my length on this cold bed.
          By day's approach, look to be visited.   430

                              [*He lies down and sleeps.*

Enter HELENA.

HELENA   O weary night, O long and tedious night,

          Abate thy hours! Shine comforts from the east,
That I may back to Athens by daylight,
      From these that my poor company detest.
And sleep, that sometimes shuts up sorrow's eye,
Steal me awhile from mine own company.
                [She lies down near Demetrius and sleeps.

ROBIN   Yet but three? Come one more.
         Two of both kinds makes up four.
         Here she comes, curst and sad.
         Cupid is a knavish lad,   440
         Thus to make poor females mad.

             Enter HERMIA.

HERMIA   Never so weary, never so in woe;
      Bedabbled with the dew and torn with briars;
I can no further crawl, no further go;
      My legs can keep no pace with my desires.
Here will I rest me till the break of day.
Heavens shield Lysander, if they mean a fray!
              [She lies down near Lysander and sleeps.

ROBIN   On the ground
             Sleep sound.
             I'll apply   450
             To your eye,
         Gentle lover, remedy.
                [He drips the juice upon Lysander's eyelids.
             When thou wak'st,
             Thou tak'st
             True delight
             In the sight
         Of thy former lady's eye:
And the country proverb known,
That every man should take his own,
In your waking shall be shown.   460
             Jack shall have Jill;
             Nought shall go ill;
The man shall have his mare again,
         And all shall be well.[86]
                      [Exit.

ACT 4, SCENE I.

Enter TITANIA *with* BOTTOM, *his ass's head garlanded with flowers;*
FAIRIES *following; and* OBERON *behind all, unseen.*

TITANIA   Come, sit thee down upon this flow'ry bed,
      While I thy amiable cheeks do coy,
  And stick musk-roses in thy sleek smooth head,
      And kiss thy fair large ears, my gentle joy.
             [They sit; she caresses him, etc.

BOTTOM   Where's Peaseblossom?

PEASE.   Ready.

BOTTOM   Scratch my head, Peaseblossom. Where's Mounsieur
  Cobweb?

COBWEB   Ready.

BOTTOM   Mounsieur Cobweb, good mounsieur, get you your 10
  weapons in your hand, and kill me a red-hipped humble-
  bee on the top of a thistle; and, good mounsieur, bring
  me the honey-bag. Do not fret yourself too much in
  the action, mounsieur; and, good mounsieur, have a
  care the honey-bag break not — I would be loath to
  have you overflown with a honey-bag, signior. Where's
  Mounsieur Mustardseed?

MUSTARD.   Ready.

BOTTOM   Give me your neaf, Mounsieur Mustardseed. Pray you,
  leave your curtsy, good mounsieur.[87]   20

MUSTARD.   What's your will?

BOTTOM   Nothing, good mounsieur, but to help Cavalery Cobweb to scratch. I must to the barber's, mounsieur, for
  methinks I am marvellous hairy about the face; and I
  am such a tender ass, if my hair do but tickle me, I
  must scratch.

TITANIA   What, wilt thou hear some music, my sweet love?

BOTTOM   I have a reasonable good ear in music. Let's have the
  tongs and the bones.[88]

TITANIA   Or say, sweet love, what thou desir'st to eat.   30

BOTTOM   Truly, a peck of provender. I could munch your good
  dry oats. Methinks I have a great desire to a bottle of
  hay. Good hay, sweet hay, hath no fellow.

TITANIA   I have a venturous fairy, that shall seek
The squirrel's hoard, and fetch thee thence new nuts.[89]

BOTTOM   I had rather have a handful or two of dried peas. But, I
pray you, let none of your people stir me; I have an
exposition of sleep come upon me.

TITANIA   Sleep thou, and I will wind thee in my arms.
Fairies, be gone, and be all ways away.[90]   40

[*Exeunt fairies.*

So doth the woodbine the sweet honeysuckle
Gently entwist;[91] the female ivy so
Enrings the barky fingers of the elm.
O, how I love thee! How I dote on thee!   [*They sleep.*

Enter ROBIN.

OBERON   Welcome, good Robin. See'st thou this sweet sight?
Her dotage now I do begin to pity.
For meeting her of late, behind the wood,
Seeking sweet favours for this hateful fool,
I did upbraid her and fall out with her.
For she his hairy temples then had rounded   50
With coronet of fresh and fragrant flowers;
And that same dew which sometime on the buds
Was wont to swell, like round and orient pearls,
Stood now within the pretty flow'rets' eyes,
Like tears that did their own disgrace bewail.
When I had at my pleasure taunted her,
And she in mild terms begged my patience,[92]
I then did ask of her her changeling child:
Which straight she gave me, and her fairy sent
To bear him to my bower in Fairyland.   60
And now I have the boy, I will undo
This hateful imperfection of her eyes.
And, gentle Puck, take this transformèd scalp
From off the head of this Athenian swain;
That he, awaking when the other do,
May all to Athens back again repair,
And think no more of this night's accidents
But as the fierce vexation of a dream.
But first I will release the Fairy Queen.

[*He drips juice upon her eyelids.*

| | Be, as thou wast wont to be: | 70 |

        Be, as thou wast wont to be: 70
        See, as thou wast wont to see.
        Dian's bud[93] o'er Cupid's flower
        Hath such force and blessèd power.
        Now, my Titania: wake you, my sweet queen.

TITANIA   My Oberon! What visions have I seen!
        Methought I was enamoured of an ass.

OBERON   There lies your love.

TITANIA   How came these things to pass?
        O, how mine eyes do loathe his visage now!

OBERON   Silence a while. Robin, take off this head.
        Titania, music call; and strike more dead   80
        Than common sleep of all these five the sense.[94]

TITANIA   Music, ho! Music: such as charmeth sleep. [*Soft music.*

ROBIN   Now, when thou wak'st, with thine own fool's
                                eyes peep.
               [*He removes the ass's head from Bottom.*

OBERON   Sound, music. [*The music becomes louder.*]
               Come, my queen, take hands with me,
        And rock the ground whereon these sleepers be.
                             [*They dance.*

        Now, thou and I are new in amity,
        And will tomorrow midnight solemnly
        Dance in Duke Theseus' house triumphantly,
        And bless it to all fair prosperity.
        There shall the pairs of faithful lovers be   90
        Wedded, with Theseus, all in jollity.

ROBIN   Fairy King, attend, and mark:
        I do hear the morning lark.

OBERON   Then, my queen, in silence sad,
        Trip we after the night's shade:[95]
        We the globe can compass soon,
        Swifter than the wand'ring moon.

TITANIA   Come my lord, and, in our flight,
        Tell me how it came this night
        That I sleeping here was found   100
        With these mortals on the ground.
               [*Exeunt Oberon, Titania and Robin.*

A sound of horns. Enter THESEUS, HIPPOLYTA,
EGEUS *and* OTHERS.

THESEUS   Go, one of you, find out the forester:
For now our observation is performed;
And since we have the vaward of the day,
My love shall hear the music of my hounds.
Uncouple in the western valley; let them go.
Dispatch, I say, and find the forester.   [*Exit man.*
We will, fair queen, up to the mountain's top,
And mark the musical confusion
Of hounds and echo in conjunction.   110

HIPPOLYTA I was with Hercules and Cadmus once,
When in a wood of Crete they bayed the bear
With hounds of Sparta:[96] never did I hear
Such gallant chiding; for – besides the groves –
The skies, the fountains, every region near,
Seemed all one mutual cry. I never heard
So musical a discord, such sweet thunder.

THESEUS   My hounds are bred out of the Spartan kind:
So flewed, so sanded; and their heads are hung
With ears that sweep away the morning dew;   120
Crook-kneed, and dewlapped like Thessalian bulls;
Slow in pursuit; but matched in mouth like bells,
Each under each.[97] A cry more tunable
Was never hollowed to,[98] nor cheered with horn,
In Crete, in Sparta, nor in Thessaly.
Judge when you hear. But, soft, what nymphs are these?

EGEUS   My lord, this is my daughter here asleep,
And this Lysander; this Demetrius is;
This Helena, old Nedar's Helena.
I wonder of their being here together.   130

THESEUS   No doubt they rose up early to observe
The rite of May; and, hearing our intent,
Came here, in grace of our solemnity.
But, speak, Egeus: is not this the day
That Hermia should give answer of her choice?

EGEUS   It is, my lord.

THESEUS   Go, bid the huntsmen wake them with their horns.
          [*A shout within. Horns sound. The lovers awake and rise.*

     Good morrow, friends. Saint Valentine is past;
     Begin these wood-birds but to couple now?[99]
LYSANDER Pardon, my lord.   [*The lovers kneel before Theseus.*
THESEUS   I pray you all, stand up.   140
     [*To Lysander and Demetrius:*]
     I know you two are rival enemies:
     How comes this gentle concord in the world,
     That hatred is so far from jealousy
     To sleep by hate, and fear no enmity?
LYSANDER My lord, I shall reply amazèdly,
     Half sleep, half waking. But as yet, I swear,
     I cannot truly say how I came here.
     But, as I think (for truly would I speak,
     And now I do bethink me, so it is),
     I came with Hermia hither. Our intent   150
     Was to be gone from Athens, where we might,
     Without the peril of th'Athenian law –
EGEUS Enough, enough, my lord; you have enough.
     I beg the law, the law, upon his head. –
     They would have stol'n away, they would, Demetrius,
     Thereby to have defeated you and me:
     You of your wife, and me of my consent,
     Of my consent that she should be your wife.
DEMETR. My lord, fair Helen told me of their stealth,
     Of this their purpose hither, to this wood,   160
     And I in fury hither followed them;
     Fair Helena in fancy following me.
     But, my good lord, I wot not by what power
     (But by some power it is), my love to Hermia,
     Melted as melts the snow,[100] seems to me now
     As the remembrance of an idle gaud
     Which in my childhood I did dote upon;
     And all the faith, the virtue of my heart,
     The object and the pleasure of mine eye,
     Is only Helena. To her, my lord,   170
     Was I betrothed ere I saw Hermia:
     But, like in sickness did I loathe this food;
     So, as in health, come to my natural taste,[101]
     Now I do wish it, love it, long for it,

And will for evermore be true to it.

THESEUS Fair lovers, you are fortunately met.
Of this discourse we more will hear anon. –
Egeus, I will overbear your will;
For in the temple, by and by, with us,
These couples shall eternally be knit.   180
And, for the morning now is something worn,
Our purposed hunting shall be set aside.
Away with us, to Athens! Three and three,
We'll hold a feast in great solemnity.
Come, Hippolyta.
          [*Exeunt Theseus, Hippolyta, Egeus and their followers.*

DEMETR. These things seem small and undistinguishable,
Like far-off mountains turnèd into clouds.

HERMIA Methinks I see these things with parted eye,
When everything seems double.

HELENA   So methinks:
And I have found Demetrius like a jewel,   190
Mine own, and not mine own.

DEMETR.   But are you sure
That we are now awake? It seems to me,
That yet we sleep, we dream. You do not think[102]
The duke was here, and bid us follow him?

HERMIA Yea, and my father.

HELENA   And Hippolyta.

LYSANDER And he did bid us follow to the temple.

DEMETR. Why then, we are awake. Let's follow him,
And by the way let us recount our dreams.
                                    [*Exeunt lovers.*

BOTTOM [*awaking:*] When my cue comes, call me, and I will
answer. My next is, 'most fair Pyramus'. Hey-ho! Peter   200
Quince? Flute, the bellows-mender? Snout, the tinker?
Starveling? God's my life! Stol'n hence, and left me
asleep! I have had a most rare vision. I have had a dream –
past the wit of man to say what dream it was. Man is but
an ass, if he go about to expound this dream. Methought
I was – there is no man can tell what. Methought I was,
and methought I had . . . But man is but a patched fool, if
he will offer to say what methought I had. The eye of

man hath not heard, the ear of man hath not seen, man's
hand is not able to taste, his tongue to conceive, nor his 210
heart to report, what my dream was.[103] I will get Peter
Quince to write a ballad of this dream: it shall be called
'Bottom's Dream', because it hath no bottom: and I will
sing it in the latter end of a play, before the duke.
Peradventure, to make it the more gracious, I shall sing it
at her death.[104]

[*Exit.*

SCENE 2.

Athens. Peter Quince's abode.

Enter QUINCE, FLUTE, SNOUT *and* STARVELING.

QUINCE   Have you sent to Bottom's house? Is he come home yet?

STARV.   He cannot be heard of. Out of doubt he is transported.

FLUTE   If he come not, then the play is marred. It goes not
forward, doth it?

QUINCE   It is not possible. You have not a man in all Athens able
to discharge Pyramus but he.

FLUTE   No, he hath simply the best wit of any handicraft man
in Athens.

QUINCE   Yea, and the best person too; and he is a very paramour
for a sweet voice.   10

FLUTE   You must say 'paragon'. A paramour is, God bless us, a
thing of naught.

Enter SNUG.

SNUG   Masters, the duke is coming from the temple, and there
is two or three lords and ladies more married. If our
sport had gone forward, we had all been made men.

FLUTE   O sweet bully Bottom! Thus hath he lost sixpence a
day during his life: he could not have 'scaped sixpence
a day. An the duke had not given him sixpence a day
for playing Pyramus, I'll be hanged. He would have
deserved it. Sixpence a day in Pyramus, or nothing.   20

Enter BOTTOM.

BOTTOM   Where are these lads? Where are these hearts?

QUINCE Bottom! O most courageous day! O most happy hour!

BOTTOM Masters, I am to discourse wonders; but ask me not what. For if I tell you, I am no true Athenian. I will tell you everything, right as it fell out.

QUINCE Let us hear, sweet Bottom.

BOTTOM Not a word of me. All that I will tell you is, that the duke hath dined. Get your apparel together, good strings to your beards, new ribbons to your pumps; meet presently at the palace; every man look o'er his part. For the short and the long is, our play is preferred. In any case, let Thisby have clean linen; and let not him that plays the lion pare his nails, for they shall hang out for the lion's claws. And, most dear actors, eat no onions nor garlic, for we are to utter sweet breath; and I do not doubt but to hear them say, it is a sweet comedy. No more words. Away, go away!

[Exeunt.

ACT 5, SCENE 1.

The hall in the palace of Duke Theseus.

Enter THESEUS *and* HIPPOLYTA, *followed by*
PHILOSTRATE, LORDS *and* ATTENDANTS.

HIPPOLYTA 'Tis strange, my Theseus, that these lovers speak of.

THESEUS   More strange than true. I never may believe
These antic fables, nor these fairy toys.
Lovers and madmen have such seething brains,
Such shaping fantasies, that apprehend
More than cool reason ever comprehends.
The lunatic, the lover and the poet
Are of imagination all compáct.
One sees more devils than vast hell can hold:
That is the madman. The lover, all as frantic,   10
Sees Helen's beauty in a brow of Egypt.[105]
The poet's eye, in a fine frenzy rolling,
Doth glance from heaven to earth, from earth to heaven;
And as imagination bodies forth
The forms of things unknown, the poet's pen
Turns them to shapes, and gives to airy nothing
A local habitation and a name.
Such tricks hath strong imagination
That, if it would but apprehend some joy,
It comprehends some bringer of that joy;   20
Or in the night, imagining some fear,
How easy is a bush supposed a bear!

HIPPOLYTA But, all the story of the night told over,
And all their minds transfigured so together,
More witnesseth than fancy's images,
And grows to something of great constancy;
But howsoever, strange and admirable.

Enter LYSANDER *with* HERMIA, DEMETRIUS *with* HELENA.

THESEUS   Here come the lovers, full of joy and mirth.
Joy, gentle friends, joy and fresh days of love
Accompany your hearts!

LYSANDER   More than to us   30

             Wait in your royal walks, your board, your bed!

THESEUS   Come now: what masques, what dances shall we have,
             To wear away this long age of three hours
             Between our after-supper and bed-time?
             Where is our usual manager of mirth?
             What revels are in hand? Is there no play
             To ease the anguish of a torturing hour?
             Call Philostrate.[106]

PHILOSTR.   Here, mighty Theseus.

THESEUS   Say, what abridgement have you for this evening?
             What masque, what music? How shall we beguile   40
             The lazy time, if not with some delight?

PHILOSTR. There is a brief how many sports are ripe.
             Make choice of which your highness will see first.

                                    [He presents a paper.

THESEUS   'The battle with the Centaurs, to be sung
             By an Athenian eunuch to the harp'?
             We'll none of that. That have I told my love,
             In glory of my kinsman Hercules.[107]
             'The riot of the tipsy Bacchanals,
             Tearing the Thracian singer in their rage'?[108]
             That is an old device; and it was played   50
             When I from Thebes came last a conqueror.
             'The thrice three Muses mourning for the death
             Of Learning, late deceased in beggary'?
             That is some satire, keen and critical,
             Not sorting with a nuptial ceremony.
             'A tedious brief scene of young Pyramus
             And his love Thisby; very tragical mirth'?
             'Merry' and 'tragical'? 'Tedious' and 'brief'?
             That is hot ice and wondrous strange snow.[109]
             How shall we find the concord of this discord?[110]   60

PHILOSTR. A play there is, my lord, some ten words long,
             Which is as brief as I have known a play;
             But by ten words, my lord, it is too long,
             Which makes it tedious: for in all the play
             There is not one word apt, one player fitted.
             And tragical, my noble lord, it is,
             For Pyramus therein doth kill himself:

Which when I saw rehearsed, I must confess,
Made mine eyes water; but more merry tears
The passion of loud laughter never shed.   70

THESEUS   What are they that do play it?

PHILOSTR. Hard-handed men that work in Athens here,
Which never laboured in their minds till now;
And now have toiled their unbreathed memories
With this same play, against your nuptial.

THESEUS   And we will hear it.

PHILOSTR.   No, my noble lord,
It is not for you. I have heard it over,
And it is nothing, nothing in the world;
Unless you can find sport in their intents,
Extremely stretched and conned with cruel pain,   -   80
To do you service.

THESEUS   I will hear that play:
For never anything can be amiss,
When simpleness and duty tender it.
Go bring them in; and take your places, ladies.

                              [*Exit Philostrate.*

HIPPOLYTA I love not to see wretchedness o'ercharged,
And duty in his service perishing.

THESEUS   Why, gentle sweet, you shall see no such thing.

HIPPOLYTA He says, they can do nothing in this kind.

THESEUS   The kinder we, to give them thanks for nothing.
Our sport shall be to take what they mistake;   90
And what poor duty cannot do, noble respect
Takes it in might, not merit.[111]
Where I have come, great clerks have purposèd
To greet me with premeditated welcomes;
Where I have seen them shiver and look pale,
Make periods in the midst of sentences,
Throttle their practised accent in their fears,
And in conclusion dumbly have broke off,
Not paying me a welcome. Trust me, sweet,
Out of this silence, yet, I picked a welcome;   100
And in the modesty of fearful duty
I read as much as from the rattling tongue
Of saucy and audacious eloquence.

Love, therefore, and tongue-tied simplicity,
In least, speak most, to my capacity.

Enter PHILOSTRATE.

PHILOSTR. So please your grace, the Prologue is addressed.
THESEUS   Let him approach.

Enter QUINCE *as Prologue.*

QUINCE   'If we offend, it is with our good will.
  That you should think, we come not to offend,
 But with good will. To show our simple skill,   110
  That is the true beginning of our end.
Consider then, we come but in despite.
 We do not come, as minding to content you,
Our true intent is. All for your delight
 We are not here. That you should here repent you,
The actors are at hand; and, by their show,
 You shall know all that you are like to know.'

          [*He stands aside.*

THESEUS   This fellow doth not stand upon points.[112]
LYSANDER   He hath rid his prologue like a rough colt: he knows
  not the stop. A good moral, my lord: it is not enough 120
  to speak, but to speak true.
HIPPOLYTA Indeed he hath played on his prologue like a child on a
  recorder: a sound, but not in government.
THESEUS   His speech was like a tangled chain: nothing impaired,
  but all disordered. Who is next?

Enter BOTTOM *as Pyramus,* FLUTE *as Thisby,* SNOUT *as Wall,*
 STARVELING *as Moonshine, and* SNUG *as Lion.*

QUINCE   'Gentles, perchance you wonder at this show,
  But wonder on, till truth make all things plain.
 This man is Pyramus, if you would know:
  This beauteous lady, Thisby is, certáin.
 This man, with lime and rough-cast, doth present 130
  Wall, that vile Wall which did these lovers sunder;
 And through Wall's chink, poor souls, they are content
  To whisper. At the which, let no man wonder.
 This man, with lantern, dog, and bush of thorn,
  Presenteth Moonshine. For, if you will know,
 By moonshine did these lovers think no scorn

       To meet at Ninus' tomb, there, there to woo.
    This grisly beast (which "Lion" hight by name)
      The trusty Thisby, coming first by night,
      Did scare away, or rather did affright;   140
    And, as she fled, her mantle she did fall,
      Which Lion vile with bloody mouth did stain.
    Anon comes Pyramus, sweet youth, and tall,
      And finds his trusty Thisby's mantle slain;
    Whereat, with blade, with bloody blameful blade,
      He bravely broached his boiling bloody breast.
    And Thisby, tarrying in mulberry shade,
      His dagger drew, and died. For all the rest,
    Let Lion, Moonshine, Wall, and lovers twain
    At large discourse, while here they do remain.'   150
              [*Exeunt all the troupe except Snout as Wall.*

THESEUS   I wonder if the lion be to speak.
DEMETR.   No wonder, my lord:
          One lion may, when many asses do.

            SNOUT *steps forward.*

SNOUT   'In this same interlude it doth befall
      That I, one Snout by name,[113] present a wall:
      And such a wall, as I would have you think,
      That had in it a crannied hole or chink:
      Through which the lovers, Pyramus and Thisby,
      Did whisper often, very secretly.
      This loam, this rough-cast and this stone doth show   160
      That I am that same wall; the truth is so.
               [*He parts his legs.*[114]
      And this the cranny is, right and sinister,
      Through which the fearful lovers are to whisper.'
THESEUS   Would you desire lime and hair to speak better?
DEMETR.   It is the wittiest partition that ever I heard discourse,
      my lord.

           Enter BOTTOM *as Pyramus.*

THESEUS   Pyramus draws near the wall: silence!
BOTTOM   'O grim-looked night, O night, with hue so black!
      O night, which ever art, when day is not;
      O night, O night, alack, alack, alack,   170

      I fear my Thisby's promise is forgot!
    And thou, O wall, O sweet, O lovely wall,
        That stand'st between her father's ground and mine,
    Thou wall, O wall, O sweet and lovely wall,
      Show me thy chink to blink through with
                            mine eyne.[115]

                          [*Wall obeys.*

    Thanks, courteous wall. Jove shield thee well for this!
      But what see I? No Thisby do I see.
    O wicked wall, through whom I see no bliss,
      Cursed be thy stones for thus deceiving me!'

THESEUS   The wall, methinks, being sensible, should curse again. 180
BOTTOM   No, in truth, sir, he should not. 'Deceiving me!' is
    Thisby's cue: she is to enter now, and I am to spy her
    through the wall. You shall see, it will fall pat as I told
    you. Yonder she comes.

                Enter FLUTE *as Thisby.*

FLUTE   'O wall, full often hast thou heard my moans,
      For parting my fair Pyramus and me.
    My cherry lips have often kissed thy stones,
      Thy stones with lime and hair knit up in thee.'

PYRAMUS 'I see a voice: now will I to the chink,
      To spy an I can hear my Thisby's face.   190
    Thisby?'

FLUTE   'My love! Thou art my love, I think.'
BOTTOM   'Think what thou wilt, I am thy lover's grace;
    And, like Limander, am I trusty still.'
FLUTE   'And I like Helen, till the Fates me kill.'
BOTTOM   'Not Shafalus to Procrus was so true.'[116]
FLUTE   'As Shafalus to Procrus, I to you.'
BOTTOM   'O kiss me, through the hole of this vile wall.'
FLUTE   'I kiss the wall's hole, not your lips at all.'
BOTTOM   'Wilt thou at Ninny's tomb meet me straightway?'
FLUTE   ''Tide life, 'tide death, I come without delay.'   200
                      [*Exeunt Bottom and Flute.*

SNOUT   'Thus have I, Wall, my part dischargèd so;
      And being done, thus Wall away doth go.'
                          [*Exit Snout.*

THESEUS   Now is the mural down[117] between the two neighbours.

DEMETR.   No remedy, my lord, when walls are so wilful to hear
            without warning.

HIPPOLYTA   This is the silliest stuff that ever I heard.

THESEUS   The best in this kind are but shadows; and the worst
            are no worse, if imagination amend them.

HIPPOLYTA   It must be *your* imagination, then, and not theirs.

THESEUS   If we imagine no worse of them than they of them-   210
            selves, they may pass for excellent men. Here come
            two noble beasts in, a man and a lion.[118]

            Enter STARVELING *as Moonshine and* SNUG *as Lion.*

SNUG   'You ladies, you, whose gentle hearts do fear
                The smallest monstrous mouse that creeps on floor,
            May now, perchance, both quake and tremble here,
                When lion rough, in wildest rage, doth roar.
            Then know that I as Snug the joiner am
            A lion fell, nor else no lion's dam.
            For if I should as lion come in strife
            Into this place, 'twere pity on my life.'   220

THESEUS   A very gentle beast, and of a good conscience.

DEMETR.   The very best at a beast, my lord, that e'er I saw.

LYSANDER   This lion is a very fox for his valour.

THESEUS   True; and a goose for his discretion.[119]

DEMETR.   Not so, my lord, for his valour cannot carry his dis-
            cretion, and the fox carries the goose.

THESEUS   His discretion, I am sure, cannot carry his valour, for
            the goose carries not the fox. It is well: leave it to his
            discretion, and let us listen to the moon.

STARV.   'This lanthorn doth the hornèd moon present' —[120]   230

DEMETR.   He should have worn the horns on his head.

THESEUS   He is no crescent, and his horns are invisible within
            the circumference.[121]

STARV.   'This lanthorn doth the hornèd moon present,
            Myself the man i'th' moon do seem to be' —

THESEUS   This is the greatest error of all the rest: the man should
            be put into the lantern. How is it else the man i'th'
            moon?

DEMETR.   He dares not come there for the candle — for, you see,
            it is already in snuff.[122]   240

HIPPOLYTA	I am aweary of this moon. Would he would change!
THESEUS	It appears, by his small light of discretion, that he is in the wane: but yet, in courtesy, in all reason, we must stay the time.
LYSANDER	Proceed, Moon.
STARV.	All that I have to say, is to tell you that the lanthorn is the moon, I the man i'th' moon, this thorn-bush my thorn-bush, and this dog my dog.
DEMETR.	Why, all these should be in the lantern; for all these are in the moon. But, silence: here comes Thisby.

                                                                    250

Enter FLUTE *as Thisby.*

FLUTE	'This is old Ninny's tomb. Where is my love?'
SNUG	[*roars:*] 'Oh!'

                              [*Thisby drops her mantle and runs off.*

DEMETR.	Well roared, Lion.
THESEUS	Well run, Thisby.
HIPPOLYTA	Well shone, Moon. Truly, the moon shines with a good grace. [*Lion gnaws Thisby's mantle.*
THESEUS	Well moused, Lion.
DEMETR.	And then came Pyramus.

Enter BOTTOM *as Pyramus; exit* SNUG *as Lion.*

LYSANDER	And so the lion vanished.
BOTTOM	'Sweet moon, I thank thee for thy sunny beams. 260

> I thank thee, moon, for shining now so bright;
> For, by thy gracious, golden, glittering gleams,
> I trust to take of truest Thisby sight.
>   But stay: O spite!
>   But mark, poor knight,
>   What dreadful dole is here!
>   Eyes, do you see?
>   How can it be?
>   O dainty duck, O dear!
>   Thy mantle good,   270
>   What, stained with blood?
>   Approach, ye Furies fell!
>   O Fates, come, come,
>   Cut thread and thrum,
>   Quail, crush, conclude, and quell!'[123]

THESEUS   This passion – and the death of a dear friend – would
go near to make a man look sad.

HIPPOLYTA Beshrew my heart, but I pity the man.

BOTTOM   'O wherefore, Nature, didst thou lions frame?
    Since lion vilde hath here deflowered my dear,[124]   280
    Which is – no, no – which *was* the fairest dame
      That lived, that loved, that liked, that looked
                   with cheer.
        Come, tears, confound;
        Out, sword, and wound
      The pap of Pyramus:
        Ay, that left pap,
        Where heart doth hop.
      Thus die I, thus, thus, thus.

                           [*He stabs himself.*

        Now am I dead,
        Now am I fled,   290
      My soul is in the sky.
        Tongue, lose thy light!
        Moon, take thy flight!   [*Exit Moonshine.*
      Now die, die, die, die, die.'   [*Pyramus dies.*

DEMETR.   No die, but an ace, for him: for he is but one.

LYSANDER   Less than an ace, man: for he is dead, he is nothing.

THESEUS   With the help of a surgeon, he might yet recover, and
prove an ass.[125]

HIPPOLYTA How chance Moonshine is gone before Thisby comes
back and finds her lover?   300

THESEUS   She will find him by starlight.

              Enter FLUTE *as Thisby.*

       Here she comes, and her passion ends the play.

HIPPOLYTA Methinks she should not use a long one for such a
Pyramus: I hope she will be brief.

DEMETR.   A mote will turn the balance, which Pyramus, which
Thisby, is the better: he for a man, God warr'nt us; she
for a woman, God bless us.

LYSANDER   She hath spied him already with those sweet eyes.

DEMETR.   And thus she means, videlicet:[126]

FLUTE   'Asleep, my love?   310
        What, dead, my dove?

        O Pyramus, arise,
           Speak, speak. Quite dumb?
           Dead, dead? A tomb
        Must cover thy sweet eyes.
           These lily lips,
           This cherry nose,
        These yellow cowslip cheeks,
           Are gone, are gone:
           Lovers, make moan;   320
        His eyes were green as leeks.
           O Sisters Three,
           Come, come, to me,
        With hands as pale as milk;
           Lay them in gore,
           Since you have shore
        With shears his thread of silk.
           Tongue, not a word;
           Come, trusty sword,
        Come, blade, my breast imbrue.   330

                       [Thisby stabs herself.

           And farewell, friends:
           Thus Thisby ends:
        Adieu, adieu, adieu.'

                         [Thisby falls.

THESEUS   Moonshine and Lion are left to bury the dead.

DEMETR.   Ay and Wall too.

BOTTOM[127] [*rising:*] No, I assure you, the wall is down that parted their fathers. Will it please you to see the Epilogue, or to hear a Bergomask dance[128] between two of our company?

THESEUS   No Epilogue, I pray you — for your play needs no 340 excuse. Never excuse; for when the players are all dead, there need none to be blamed. Marry, if he that writ it had played Pyramus and hanged himself in Thisby's garter, it would have been a fine tragedy — and so it is truly, and very notably discharged. But come, your Bergomask; let your Epilogue alone.

        BOTTOM *and* FLUTE[129] *dance the Bergomask
            and exeunt.* THESEUS *rises.*

The iron tongue of midnight hath told twelve.
Lovers, to bed; 'tis almost fairy time.
I fear we shall outsleep the coming morn
As much as we this night have overwatched.   350
This palpable-gross play hath well beguiled
The heavy gait of night. Sweet friends, to bed.
A fortnight hold we this solemnity,
In nightly revels and new jollity.

[*Exeunt.*

Enter ROBIN, *holding a broom.*

ROBIN   Now the hungry lion roars,
                   And the wolf behowls the moon,[130]
               Whilst the heavy ploughman snores,
                   All with weary task foredoone.[131]
               Now the wasted brands do glow,
                   Whilst the screech-owl, screeching loud,   360
               Puts the wretch that lies in woe
                   In remembrance of a shroud.[132]
               Now it is the time of night
                   That the graves, all gaping wide,
               Every one lets forth his sprite,
                   In the church-way paths to glide.
               And we fairies, that do run
                   By the triple Hecate's team
               From the presence of the sun,
                   Following darkness like a dream,[133]   370
               Now are frolic. Not a mouse
               Shall disturb this hallowed house.
               I am sent with broom before,[134]
               To sweep the dust behind the door.

Enter OBERON *and* TITANIA *with their* RETINUE.

OBERON   Through the house give glimmering light.
                    By the dead and drowsy fire,
                Every elf and fairy sprite
                    Hop as light as bird from briar;
                And this ditty after me
                Sing, and dance it trippingly.   380
TITANIA   First rehearse your song by rote;

To each word a warbling note;
Hand in hand, with fairy grace,
Will we sing and bless this place.

OBERON *leads and all the fairies sing in chorus;[135] as they sing,*
they take hands and dance about the hall. The dance ends.

OBERON   Now, until the break of day,
Through this house each fairy stray.
To the best bride-bed will we,
Which by us shall blessèd be:
And the issue there create
Ever shall be fortunate.   390
So shall all the couples three
Ever true in loving be;
And the blots of nature's hand
Shall not in their issue stand.
Never mole, hare-lip, nor scar,
Nor mark prodigious, such as are
Despisèd in nativity,
Shall upon their children be.
With this field-dew consecrate,
Every fairy take his gait,   400
And each several chamber bless,
Through this palace, with sweet peace;
And the owner of it blest
Ever shall in safety rest.
      Trip away;
      Make no stay;
Meet me all by break of day.

                              [*Exeunt all except Robin.*

ROBIN   If we shadows have offended,
Think but this, and all is mended:
That you have but slumbered here   410
While these visions did appear.
And this weak and idle theme
No more yielding but a dream.[136]
Gentles, do not reprehend:
If you pardon, we will mend.
And, as I am an honest puck,

If we have unearnèd luck
Now to 'scape the serpent's tongue,
We will make amends, ere long;[137]
Else the puck a liar call.   420
So, good night unto you all.
Give me your hands, if we be friends,
And Robin shall restore amends.

NOTES ON *A MIDSUMMER NIGHT'S DREAM*

In these notes, the abbreviations used include the following:

e.g.:	*exempli gratia* (for example);
F1:	First Folio, 1623;
FC:	Fausto Cercignani: *Shakespeare's Works and Elizabethan Pronunciation* (Oxford: Oxford University Press, 1981);
HK:	Helge Kökeritz: *Shakespeare's Pronunciation* (New Haven, Conn.: Yale University Press, 1953);
i.e.:	*id est* (that is);
O.E.D.:	*The Oxford English Dictionary* (Oxford: Oxford University Press, 1989);
PH:	*A Midsummer Night's Dream*, ed. Peter Holland (Oxford: Oxford University Press, 1994; reprinted 1998);
Q1:	First Quarto, 1600;
S.D.:	stage direction.

In the case of a pun or an ambiguity, the meanings are distinguished as (a) and (b).

1 (1.1. S.D.) *HIPPOLYTA*: Chaucer's 'The Knight's Tale' (in *The Canterbury Tales*) transmits the legend that Duke Theseus, ruler of Athens, conquered the Amazons and their realm, and married their queen, Hippolyta. ('The Knight's Tale' also provided the name 'Philostrate'.)

2 (1.1.2–4) *four happy days . . . wanes!*: The ensuing action seems to span two days and an intervening night, not four days. The time of a new moon was traditionally thought to be auspicious for the occasion of a marriage.

3 (1.1.10) *New-bent*: Q1 and F1 have 'Now bent'; but, as the time described is the future, the emendation 'New-bent' seems appropriate.

4 (1.1.27) *This man . . . child*: The Second Folio (1632) regularised the metre of this line by changing 'This man' to 'This'. Alternative modes of regularisation include reducing 'bewitched' to 'witched' and compressing 'bewitched' to 'b'witched'.

5 (1.1.32) *stol'n . . . fantasy*: 'stolen from Demetrius the imprinting of her amatory imagination' (which now displays Lysander's image instead of Demetrius's).

6 (1.1.76–8) *But earthlier . . . blessedness*: Shakespeare's sonnets 5 and 6 emphasise that the young man should live on by marrying to produce children: thus he will resemble 'flowers distilled' (as perfume). Such flowers, 'though they with winter meet, / Lose but their show; their substance still lives sweet.'

7 (1.1.89–90) *Or on . . . life*: Diana, one incarnation of the moon-goddess, was patroness of chastity.

8 (1.1.124) *I must . . . business*: The line is metrically regular, as 'business' is here trisyllabic ('busy-ness').

9 (1.1.149) *confusion*: tetrasyllabic ('con-fú-si-òn'), to preserve the metre, like 'dissension' ('dis-sén-si-òn') at 2.1.116 and 'derision' ('de-rís-i-òn') at 3.2.197.

10 (1.1.152) *patience*: trisyllabic, to preserve the metre.

11 (1.1.167) *To do . . . May*: Traditionally, May was celebrated in games and in overnight revelries. In 1583 Philip Stubbes alleged that when a hundred virgins went to the woods for this purpose, scarcely a third of them returned 'undefiled'.

12 (1.1.173–4) *by that fire . . . seen*: Virgil's *Aeneid* and Marlowe's *Dido* tell how Dido, Queen of Carthage, was deserted by her lover, Aeneas, after which she committed suicide on a pyre.

13 (1.1.187) *Your words I catch*: Both Q1 and F1 give this phrase. (The idea is that though Helena can grasp Hermia's sense, she cannot emulate Hermia's melodious utterance or bright eyes.) Some editors substitute 'Yours [i.e. your "favour", your attractiveness] would I catch'.

14 (1.1.226) *How . . . be!*: 'How happy some people can be, compared to others!'

15 (1.1.232) *holding no quantity*: probably 'containing no worthwhile substance'.

16 (1.1.249) *it is a dear expense*: 'it will be costly to me'.

17 (1.2. S.D.) QUINCE . . . STARVELING: The name 'Quince' suggests 'acidic fruit of the pear family' but is probably, here, a version of 'quines' or 'quoins', which could aptly mean 'wooden wedges used by carpenters'. A 'bottom' was the core or spool on which a weaver's skein of thread or yarn was wound. The adjective 'snug' can mean close-fitting, and Snug, being a joiner, should make close-fitting joints. Flute, being a bellows-mender, might repair fluted church-organs (and his voice may be a fluty treble). The noun 'snout' can mean 'spout', and thus is appropriate for Snout, a tinker who could mend kettles. Tailors were proverbially deemed thin: hence the name 'Starveling', implying a thin, weak person.

18 (1.2.11) *Pyramus and Thisby*: Ovid's *Metamorphoses* (Bk. 4) tells how Pyramus and Thisby (or Thisbe) lived next door to each other. They fell in love, but their parents forbade marriage, so that they were obliged to communicate through a chink in the party wall. They agreed to escape and to meet at the tomb of Ninus. While Thisby waited there, a lioness with bloodstained jaws approached; and, when Thisby ran away, dropping her veil, the beast gnawed it, leaving it marked with blood. Pyramus arrived, found the stained veil, and, assuming that Thisby had been killed, slew himself with a sword. Next, Thisby emerged, and, on discovering Pyramus' corpse, lamented at length, and finally used his weapon to kill herself. Pyramus' blood caused a nearby mulberry tree to bear, thenceforth, purple fruit. The parents, penitent, let the lovers' ashes rest in a single urn. (The plot has resemblances to that of *Romeo and Juliet*.)

19 (1.2.25–32) *'The raging . . . Fates'*: a burlesque of the kind of writing found in John Studley's translation of Seneca's *Hercules Oetæus*.

20 (1.2.45) *'Thisny? Thisny?'*: This may be intended as a pet-name version of 'Thisby'. Q1 and F1 have '*Thisne, Thisne,*'.

21 (1.2.83–6) *French-crown-colour . . . barefaced*: Bottom refers to the golden colour of the French crown, a coin; Quince refers punningly to the bald heads of Frenchmen afflicted by syphilis (the 'French disease').

22 (1.2.98) *hold . . . bow-strings*: 'Remain resolute, or suffer disgrace' (the idea probably being that bowmen in defeat would cut their bow-strings).

23 (2.1. S.D.) Night . . . FAIRY: Q1 has: 'Enter a Fairie at one doore, and Robin goodfellow at another.' F1 has the same wording. This usefully indicates the early staging. 'Robin Goodfellow' was the traditional propitiatory name of a devilish or mischievous figure of folklore. (In the anonymous play Grim the Collier of Croydon, the devil Akercock takes the name 'Robin Goodfellow' when he ascends to live among mortals.) A puck is a representative of a type of hobgoblin, a malicious or evil spirit. The term has such variants as 'pooka' or 'pouke' (recalling 'spook'), and Spenser refers to 'the Pouke' as an evil sprite. Shakespeare seems to have made the type unusually benign. In A Midsummer Night's Dream, the term 'puck' usually functions as a generic noun; but occasionally it seems to serve as an alternative proper noun for Robin, and there I capitalise it as 'Puck'.

24 (2.1.7) moon's sphere: The short line fits the sense; but, should regularity be desired, the metre and rhyme become sufficiently regular if 'sphere' is pronounced disyllabically, approximately as 'sfee-air'. (Some editors prefer to lengthen 'moon's' to 'moonës'.) 'The moon's sphere' is the rotating transparent globe in which, according to the ancient Ptolemaic cosmology, the moon was fixed.

25 (2.1.9) her orbs . . . green: fairy rings: circles of grass darkened by decayed fungi.

26 (2.1.23) a changeling: normally, the fairy offspring left in exchange when the fairies stole a human baby, but here, unusually, the stolen mortal child. 'Changeling' is trisyllabic here ('change-a-ling') but disyllabic at line 120.

27 (2.1.48) roasted crab: a roasted crab-apple, an ingredient in a spiced drink.

28 (2.1.54) 'Tailor!' cries: perhaps because a tailor sits to work; or perhaps the cry is an equivalent to 'My bum!', because 'tail' could mean 'posterior'.

29 (2.1.58) But . . . Oberon: The line seems to be one syllable short. Some editors lengthen 'fairy' to 'faëry'; others change 'room' to 'make room'. Another solution is to stretch 'here', so that it sounds like 'hee-er'.

30 (2.1. S.D.) Enter . . . her RETINUE: Q1 has: 'Enter the King of Fairies, at one doore, with his traine; and the Queene, at another, with hers.' F1 has the same wording.

31 (2.1.66, 68) *Corin* and *Phillida*: conventional names, in the tradition of pastoral verse, for the young and amorous shepherd and shepherdess.

32 (2.1.78–80) *Perigouna, Aegles, Ariadne, Antiopa*: According to the legend, Theseus killed the father of Perigenia (or Perigouna) and copulated with her, having promised to treat her gently. He then married her off to Deloneus. 'Aegles' (spelt 'Eagles' in Q1 and F1) was originally 'Aegle', the name of a nymph who, loved by Theseus, caused him to abandon Ariadne on Naxos. Before this treachery, Ariadne had fallen in love with Theseus and provided him with the thread by which he could extricate himself from the Cretan labyrinth after killing the Minotaur. Antiopa was an Amazon who, according to some versions of the legend, was abducted and raped by Theseus. Later, he abandoned her and married Phaedra.

33 (2.1.98) *nine men's morris*: a game resembling large-scale noughts and crosses. When it was played out of doors, its pattern of concentric squares could be marked in turf.

34 (2.1.99) *quaint . . . green*: maze-patterns, cut in turf or otherwise marked out, were used for games and races.

35 (2.1.101) *cheer*: an editorial emendation of 'heere' in Q1 and F1.

36 (2.1.109) *on old Hiems' . . . crown*: 'on the sparse-haired and icy top of old Winter's head'. Where Q1 and F1 have 'chinne', editors now usually substitute 'thin'.

37 (2.1.149–54) *Since once . . . music*: This passage recalls partly the legend of Arion, the musician who was saved from drowning by a dolphin, and partly the mythical sirens, the sea-nymphs whose songs could seduce voyagers. There may also be an allusion to recent history. When Queen Elizabeth visited Kenilworth in 1575, the spectacular entertainments included not only the enactment of Arion on the dolphin but also a mermaid and fireworks like glittering stars.

38 (2.1.155–64) *That very . . . fancy-free*: The 'fair vestal' and 'imperial vot'ress' is generally taken to be Elizabeth, the Virgin Queen. In this allegoric account of an unsuccessful love-suit, Cupid's arrow is extinguished by the moonbeams because the moon-goddess guards chastity.

39 (2.1.168) *'Love-in-Idleness'*: the pansy. Proverbially, 'love is the fruit of idleness'.

40 (2.1.192) *and wood*: (a) 'and mad with rage'; (b, possibly) 'and wooed'. Q1 has 'and wodde'; F1 has 'and wood'.

41 (2.1.195–8) *You . . . follow you*: 'You attract me, for, like adamant, you are magnetic as well as hard-hearted; but what you attract is not iron but steel, my heart being (proverbially) as true as steel. If you relinquish your power to attract me, I shall no longer have the power to follow you.'

42 (2.1.231) *Apollo . . . chase*: With lustful intent, the god Apollo pursued Daphne, a chaste nymph; but she prayed for divine aid and was accordingly transformed into a laurel-tree.

43 (2.1.249) *I know . . . blows*: Q1 and F1 have 'I know a banke where the wilde thyme blows'. There, the line is metrically defective, being one syllable short. Alexander Pope first regularised it by converting 'where' to 'whereon'.

44 (2.2.13) *Philomele*: The legendary Philomela was raped by her brother-in-law, Tereus; but subsequently she was transformed into a nightingale, a bird celebrated for melodious nocturnal song.

45 (2.2.54) *Love . . . conference*: 'When lovers talk, loving meanings should be assumed': i.e. 'don't misunderstand me: that's unkind'.

46 (2.2.85) *Near . . . kill-courtesy*: The irregular line may be read as tetrameter if 'courtesy' be shortened to 'court'sy', or as inconsistent pentameter if 'Near' be treated as disyllabic.

47 (3.1.22–4) *eight and six, eight and eight*: 'Eight and six' is the standard ballad metre, in which octosyllabic lines (in tetrameter, i.e. with four stresses) alternate with hexasyllabics (in trimeter, three stresses). 'Eight and eight' is the metre of some ballads; and, in any case, 'Bottom always veers to excess' (PH, p. 178).

48 (3.1.61–2) *hold . . . thus*: The best way of reconciling this suggestion with the bawdy innuendoes of 5.1.175–98 is to assume that the player of Wall uses his thumb and fingers to make a circular shape positioned between his parted legs.

49 (3.1.86) *Most . . . Jew*: 'Brisky juvenal' means 'sprightly juvenile' (though PH substitutes 'bristly' for the 'brisky' of Q1 and F1). Editors find 'lovely Jew' puzzling, speculating that 'Jew' may be an abbreviation of 'juvenile' or 'jewel', or perhaps even, occasionally, 'a term of endearment'.

50 (3.1.89) *'Ninus' tomb', man!*: In Greek mythology, Ninus was King of Assyria and the eponymous founder of Nineveh (a city sometimes called Ninus).

51   (3.1. s.d.) ass-headed: Among various sources and analogues, Reginald Scot's *Discoverie of Witchcraft* (1584) refers to the belief that an ass's head could be magically imposed on a man's shoulders, and tells how a Cypriot witch converted an English voyager into an ass for three years. *The Historie of the Damnable Life, and Deserued Death of Doctor Iohn Faustus* (a translation by 'P. F.', 1592) tells how Faustus put an ass's head on each of various victims.

52   (3.1.94) *'If . . . thine'*:   The comma after 'fair' tallies with Q1 and F1, though logically it should come after 'If I were' (thereby improving the line's scansion). The illogicality, however, may well be Bottom's.

53   (3.1.119–21) *The plain-song . . . 'nay'*:   The cuckoo's cry is ominous for married men, being a reminder that they may be cuckolded by their wives. (The connection between the cuckoo and the cuckold is that the bird's young are reared unsuspectingly by other birds in their nests, just as another man's offspring may unsuspectingly be raised by the cuckolded husband.) The song is ironically apt, if we assume that Bottom and Titania later copulate.

54   (3.1.146–7) *I will . . . go*:   Later, Milton's *Paradise Lost* (Bk. 8) will explain that when spirits embrace, a perfect merging ensues: 'Total they mix' and 'obstacle find none / Of membrane, joint, or limb'.

55   (3.1.148) *Moth*:   Q1 and F1 spell the name 'Moth', but (as in the case of Moth in *Love's Labour's Lost*) Shakespeare evidently had in mind a mote (speck), recalling Matthew 7:3 and Luke 6:41. FC adds that 'the proper name *Moth* . . . may well have been a form of *mote*, but in that case it was pronounced . . . *mot* rather than *mote*' (p. 120).

56   (3.1.149) *Ready . . . go?*:   Q1 ascribes to '*Fairies*' the words: 'Readie: and I, and I, and I. Where shall we goe?'; F1 differs little. Editors customarily divide the line, variously allocating its parts.

57   (3.1.161–64) *Hail . . . Hail!*:   Q1 and F1 allocate to '1 *Fai.*' the words 'Haile mortall, haile', to '2. *Fai.*' the word 'Haile', and to '3. *Fai.*' the word 'Haile' again. Editors usually do some redistribution here.

58   (3.1.165) *I cry . . . heartily*:   'I sincerely beg your pardon, gentlemen.' (Perhaps he has brayed a response to their greetings.)

59 (3.1.171, 2, 3) *Peaseblossom, Squash, Peascod*: 'Peaseblossom' means 'blossom of the pea-plant', 'squash' means 'unripe pea-pod', and 'peascod' means 'ripe pea-pod'.

60 (3.1.185) *enforcèd chastity*:   In this context, the words mean 'virginity violated by force', not 'person forced to remain chaste'.

61 (3.2.9) *rude mechanicals*:   'coarse workmen'. Some editors prefer 'artisans', but Shakespeare was more derogatory, referring (in *2 Henry VI*) to a 'most mechanical and dirty hand' and a 'base dunghill villain and mechanical'.

62 (3.2.25) *at one stamp*:   i.e., 'at one stamp of my foot', this being presumably an action to effect magic. Q1 and F1 have 'at our stampe', but the plural seems wrong; some editors substitute 'at a stamp' or 'at our stump'. Scot's *Discoverie of Witchcraft* says that Robin Goodfellow would decline to tread or stamp ('stampen') at houses which displeased him.

63 (3.2.28) *Made-senseless things*:   Q1 and F1 have 'Made senselesse things', presumably meaning 'things which were inanimate when originally created'.

64 (3.2.44) *Lay . . . foe*:   'vent such bitter words on your bitter enemy'.

65 (3.2.61) *As . . . sphere*:   'as the planet Venus [also known as Vesperus, the bright "evening star"], up there in her shimmering sphere'.

66 (3.2.80) *And from . . . so*:   Q1 and F1 have, on one line: 'And from thy hated presence part I: see me no more'. Editors customarily add 'so', while moving 'see me no more' to the next line, to restore the rhyme and metre.

67 (3.2.92–3) *Then fate . . . oath on oath*:   'Then fate prevails, so that [*or* Then fate decrees that] for every man who is true in love, a million fail, breaking solemn promise after solemn promise.'

68 (3.2.94, 95) *wind, find*:   At that time, 'wind' sounded like 'wined', and thus truly rhymed with 'find'.

69 (3.2.97) *With . . . dear*:   Sighs were supposed to vaporise blood. (The combination of a plural noun with a singular verb – 'sighs' with 'costs' – is not unusual in Shakespeare's work.)

70 (3.2.141) *That . . . snow*:   The line is regular if 'congealed' be trisyllabic (pronounced 'con-*jee*-uld' or 'con-*jee*-led'). 'Taurus' is a mountain-range in Turkey.

71 (3.2.188) *fiery . . . light*:   The term 'oes', generally meaning 'circles', could refer to spangles on clothing; and here the 'oes'

and 'eyes' (obviously punning on the vowels O and I) are the planets and stars in the nocturnal sky.

72 (3.2.201) *For . . . forgot?*: Q1 and F1 have 'For parting vs; O, is all forgot?', which seems one syllable short. Some editors add a word (e.g. 'this' after 'is'); others suggest that the gap may be filled by a pause before 'O', or (the best of these options) by lengthening the 'O'. Hence, here, the substitution of 'O, O!' for 'O'.

73 (3.2.212–14) *one heart . . . crest*: 'Coats in heraldry' are coats of arms, which are 'due but to one' in the sense that each is granted to only one person. 'Of the first' is a heraldic term referring to first colour specified, normally that of the ground or basis of the design; but here the phrase refers to the bodies of Hermia and Helena. They share 'one heart', likened to the single crest on the coat of arms, which sometimes depicted a hart. (Q1 has 'Two of the first life coats in heraldry', which could be interpreted as 'Two of the first living coats of arms in the history of heraldry'.)

74 (3.2.220) *I am . . . words*: Q1 has 'I am amazed at your words'; F1 has 'I am amazed at your passionate words'. Editors sometimes emend this to 'Helen, I am amazèd at your words'. The present version scans reasonably if 'passionate' be read as disyllabic ('*pash*-net'), a reading supported by FC, p. 280.

75 (3.2.237) *Ay, do!*: Q1 has 'I doe.'; F1 has 'I, doe,'. The former permits 'I do!' as an alternative to 'Ay, do!'.

76 (3.2.257–8) *No . . . loose*: In Q1, Demetrius says: 'No, no: heele / Seeme to breake loose'. In F1, his words are: 'No, no, Sir, seeme to breake loose'. Editors offer numerous emendations, notably Gary Taylor's 'No, no, sir, yield. Seem to break loose'. In the present line 257, 'Ethiop' is virtually disyllabic ('*Eeth*-yop').

77 (3.2.264) *Out . . . hence!*: Q1 has: 'Out loathed medcine: ô hated potion hence.' Some editors render this as 'Out, loathèd med'cine; O hated potion, hence.'; but this makes the line too long. (F1 substitutes 'poison' for 'potion'.)

78 (3.2.279) *Therefore . . . doubt*: Q1 and F1 have: 'Therefore be out of hope, of question, of doubt:'. The metre becomes regular if the third 'of' be deleted.

79 (3.2.282) *O me . . . canker-blossom*: 'Juggler' may be read as trisyllabic, which reduces the irregularity of the line. (Q1 has: 'O mee, you iuggler, you canker blossome,'.)

80 (3.2.288) *Fie . . . puppet, you!*: Hermia is termed 'a counterfeit' because she is seen as fraudulent, and 'a puppet' because she is

small (and perhaps manipulable). 'The differing heights of the two boy actors is used again in *As You Like It* to contrast Rosalind and Celia' (PH, p. 203).

81 (3.2.380) *Aurora's harbinger*.   Venus Phosphorus, the 'Morning Star', herald of Aurora, the dawn–goddess.

82 (3.2.389–93) *I, with . . . streams*:   The gist is: 'I can remain even until the morning sun has gilded the ocean.' Line 389 means either (a) 'I have often gone hunting with Cephalus, the lover of Aurora', or (b) 'I have often played teasingly with amorous Aurora'.

83 (3.2.399) *Goblin*:   Robin himself.

84 (3.2.406) *Speak . . . bush?*:   Q1 has 'Speake in some bush.'; F1 has 'Speake in some bush:'.

85 (3.2.421) *Ho . . . not?*:   To regularise the metre, I have added a fourth 'ho' to the three in Q1 and F1.

86 (3.2.461–4) *Jack . . . well*:   Robin cites proverbs of which the varying forms include: 'All shall be well and Jack shall have Jill'; 'All is well and the man has his mare again' ('mare' being a female partner). Given that in this play a female has had her ass, the notion that a man has a 'mare' may seem less unjust.

87 (4.1.20) *leave . . . mounsieur*.   'Leave your curtsy' means probably 'stop bowing' and possibly 'cease your courteous display'. 'Mounsieur' probably represents Bottom's pronunciation of the French 'Monsieur' ('Sir').

88 (4.1.28–9) *the tongs . . . bones*:   rudimentary instruments: tongs struck with a key and clappers rattled with the fingers.

89 (4.1.35) *The squirrel's . . . nuts*:   'Thence' (absent from Q1 and F1) is a common editorial addition to restore the metre; some editors prefer 'off'.

90 (4.1.40) *all ways away*:   Q1 and F1 have 'alwaies away', but, as she does not intend to lose her retinue permanently, the emendation (meaning 'scattered') seems correct.

91 (4.1.41–2) *the woodbine . . . entwist*:   At 2.1.251, the 'luscious woodbine' is evidently honeysuckle, as 'luscious' is inappropriate for bindweed; but here 'woodbine' must be bindweed (convolvulus). (O.E.D. says that in this period, 'woodbine' could mean 'honey-suckle', 'convolvulus' and 'ivy'.)

92 (4.1.57) *patience*:   trisyllabic, to preserve the metre.

93 (4.1.72) *Dian's bud*: Scholars are not certain of the identity of the plant which yields the restorative eye-drops. One possibility is *Artemisa vulgaris* (mugwort), as Artemis is another name of Diana, goddess of chastity.

94 (4.1.81) *Than . . . sense*: Q1 has 'Then common sleepe: of these, fine the sense.' F1 substitutes a semi-colon for the colon, but otherwise is the same as Q1. Numerous editors change 'fine' to 'five', alter the punctuation, and add 'all' to restore the metre. The 'five' are Bottom and the two pairs of lovers.

95 (4.1.95) *after . . . shade*: Q1 has 'after nights shade'; F1 has 'after the nights shade'. Some editors prefer 'after nightës shade'.

96 (4.1.111–13) *I was . . . Sparta*: Hercules was the legendary god of strength and bravery; Cadmus was the legendary founder of Thebes. Hunting-dogs of Crete and Sparta were renowned.

97 (4.1.122–3) *Slow . . . each*: The selection of hunting-dogs for their harmonious music is lengthily advocated by Gervase Markham's *Countrey Contentments* (1615).

98 (4.1.124) *hollowed to*: Q1 has 'hollowd to'; F1 has 'hallowed to'. The phrase means 'yelled at', the verb being a counterpart to 'hollered' in subsequent colloquial American.

99 (4.1.138–9) *Saint Valentine . . . now?*: St. Valentine's Day (February 14th, the day of love-declarations) was thought to be the day when birds chose their mates.

100 (4.1.164–5) *my love . . . snow*: Q1 and F1 place the line-divisions immediately after 'love' ('loue,' in Q1, 'loue' in F1) and before 'seems' ('Seemes', 'Seems'). Q1 has 'melted as the snowe'; F1 has 'melted as the snow'. Here, 'Melted as melts the snow' repairs the metre.

101 (4.1.172–3) *But . . . taste*: Q1 has 'But, like a sicknesse, did I loath this foode. / But, as in health, come to my naturall taste,'. F1 is virtually identical. The emendation clarifies matters.

102 (4.1.191–3) *But . . . think*: Q1 has 'Are you sure / That we are awake? It seemes to me, / That yet we sleepe, we dreame. Do not you thinke,'. F1 has 'It seemes to mee, / That yet we sleepe, we dreame. Do not you thinke,'. My emendations restore the metre and logic. 'You do not think' is preferable to 'Do not you think', because, as Demetrius suspects that his dream is continuing, he will suppose that the others will *not* think that the duke was there.

103 (4.1.208–11) *The eye . . . dream was*:   Bottom is confusedly recalling I Corinthians 2:9. In the Geneva Bible, the text is: 'But as it is written, The things which eye hathe not sene, nether eare hathe heard, nether came into man's heart, *are*, which God hathe prepared for them that loue him.'

104 (4.1.216) *at her death*:   perhaps he means 'at Thisby's death', or perhaps the phrase is a corruption of 'after death', meaning 'after Pyramus' death'.

105 (5.1.11) *Sees . . . Egypt*:   'sees the beauty of a Helen of Troy in someone as dark-browed as an Egyptian'. (The term 'Egyptian' connoted 'gypsy' and brings to mind Shakespeare's dark-skinned Cleopatra: Antony serves 'a gypsy's lust'.)

106 (5.1.38) *Call Philostrate*:   Q1 has 'Call *Philostrate*'; F1 has 'Call *Egeus*', and thenceforth distributes Philostrate's speeches (with one exception) to Egeus and Lysander. I prefer Q1's arrangement, which in various respects seems more consistent.

107 (5.1.44–7) *'The battle . . . Hercules*:   Ovid's *Metamorphoses*, Book 12, tells how the centaurs rioted at a wedding-feast and Theseus helped to defeat them. Hercules also took part in the battle.

108 (5.1.48–9) *'The riot . . . rage'?*:   Ovid's *Metamorphoses*, Book 11, tells how Orpheus, the Thracian poet and singer, was torn apart by the Maenads, female devotees of Bacchus.

109 (5.1.59) *That is . . . snow*:   To restore the metre, 'wondrous' (customarily disyllabic in Shakespeare) could be pronounced trisyllabically as 'wonderous'. PH (p. 234) prefers to add 'black', thus: 'wondrous strange black snow'.

110 (5.1.60) *concord . . . discord*:   echoing the Latin, *concordia discors* ('harmonious discord': Horace: *Epistles*, Bk. 1, Epistle 2, line 19).

111 (5.1.91–2) *noble . . . merit*:   'noble valuation accepts by virtue of the effort rather than of the worth'.

112 (5.1.118) *doth not . . . points*:   (a) 'is not punctilious'; (b) 'does not pause at full stops'.

113 (5.1.155) *Snout by name*:   Q1 wrongly gives Flute's name here; F1 correctly substitutes Snout's.

114 (5.1. s.d.) *He parts his legs*:   The bawdy innuendoes that ensue here make full sense only if the lovers are striving to communicate through Wall's parted legs. At 5.1.187–8, for instance, the joke depends on our recognition that 'stones' could mean 'testicles',

just as, at 5.1.197–8, it depends on the more obvious notion that 'hole' could mean 'anus'. (Thisby crouches or kneels behind Wall, speaking to Pyramus who is in front.) 'Right and sinister' (5.1.162) could refer to his right and left legs. At 3.1.61–2, Bottom had said that Wall should 'hold his fingers' so as to make a chink; so perhaps, in addition, Wall's fingers form an 'O' shape positioned between his opened thighs.

115 (5.1.168–75) *O . . . eyne*: In its repeated use of 'O', this passage parodies the rhetorical excesses of numerous Elizabethan works, among them Thomas Kyd's *Spanish Tragedy*, Shakespeare's *Romeo and Juliet* (particularly part of Act 4, scene 5) and the translation of Lodovico Dolce's *Jocasta* by George Gascoigne and Francis Kinwelmershe.

116 (5.1.193–5) *like Limander . . . true*: Bottom and Flute mangle the names. 'Limander' is the legendary Leander, who swam the Hellespont nightly to visit his beloved Hero, and eventually drowned. (Here the name is probably confused with 'leman', meaning 'lover'.) Flute should say not 'Helen' but 'Hero', as Hero was faithful but Helen eloped adulterously with Paris from her husband, Menelaus. Cephalus (here 'Shafalus'), abducted by Aurora, remained faithful to his wife, Procris ('Procrus'), and was eventually re-united with her. In another part of the legend, he wrongly accused her of infidelity; later she, hearing that *he* was unfaithful, hurried to find him and was accidentally killed by his javelin.

117 (5.1.203) *Now . . . down*: Q1 has 'Now is the Moon used'; F1 has 'Now is the morall downe'.

118 (5.1.212) *two . . . lion*: Q1 has 'two noble beasts, in a man and a Lyon'; F1 is very similar. Some editors substitute 'moon' for 'man'.

119 (5.1.223–4) *This lion . . . discretion*: The lion is famed for valour, the fox for cunning and the goose for stupidity.

120 (5.1.230) *This . . . present*: The spelling 'lanthorne' (in Q1 and F1) makes a pun with 'hornèd moon'. (At that time, a lantern's sides were usually made from transparent sheets of horn instead of glass.)

121 (5.1.231–3) *He should . . . circumference*: 'He should have worn the horns on his head, as a cuckolded husband does.' 'But only a crescent moon has visible horns (at its extremities), and he is no crescent. His horns are invisible, as he represents a full moon.'

122 (5.1.239–40) *He dares . . . snuff*: 'He dares not go inside because of the candle, for he might be burned, and in any case the candle is "in snuff" – it is (a) in danger of smouldering out, and (b) angry.'

123 (5.1.272–5) *Approach . . . quell!'*:   The Furies (vengeful female deities) arose from the underworld to pursue and punish the guilty. The Fates (Clotho, Lachesis and Atropos) were three goddesses: Clotho spun the thread representing a person's life, Lachesis drew it out, and Atropos cut it. The 'thrum' is the remainder attached to a loom when a piece of cloth is cut off. Bottom, a weaver, would have a professional interest.

124 (5.1.280) *deflowered my dear*:   He confuses 'devoured' with 'deflowered' (i.e. 'deprived of virginity'), but 'dear' is probably a deliberate pun on 'deer'.

125 (5.1.295–8) *No die . . . ass*: A 'die' is one of a pair of dice. The 'ace' is the side of a die which bears one spot (the lowest value). Demetrius seems to mean that instead of being a complete die with all its numerical faces, Pyramus is only the one-spot side, for he is now alone. Theseus remarks that he might eventually be restored as an ass (punning on 'ace'). HK (p. 89) claims that 'ace' was pronounced with a short 'a' and sounded the same as 'ass', but FC (p. 179) declares that 'the word-play rests on antithesis rather than identity'.

126 (5.1.309) *thus . . . videlicet*:   O.E.D. lists 'moans' and 'laments' (which fit here) as meanings of 'means'. (Some editors emend the word to 'moans', though Q1 and F1 give 'meanes'.) 'Videlicet' (Latin) means 'it is permissible to see'; here, 'observe the example that follows', or simply 'specifically'.

127 (5.1.336) BOTTOM: Q1 erroneously attributes this speech to '*Lyon*'; F1 corrects the error.

128 (5.1.338) *hear . . . dance*: Scholars, though unsure of the nature of a 'Bergomask' (often spelt 'Bergamask'), predominantly regard it as clownishly rustic, perhaps resembling a morris dance, and possibly accompanied by song. The name may derive from Bergamo in Italy.

129 (5.1. S.D.) BOTTOM and FLUTE: Bottom and Flute are the only two of the 'Pyramus and Thisby' cast remaining in sight, so the dance seems to be theirs. Q1 and F1 provide no stage direction here.

130 (5.1.356) *behowls the moon*:   Q1 and F1 have 'beholds the
Moone', but 'behowls' is a plausible emendation to complete a
sequence of sounds from 'roars' to 'snores'.

131 (5.1.358) *foredoone*:   Q1 has 'foredoone'; F1 has 'fore-done'. The
meaning is probably 'worn out, exhausted' ('done for'). The
archaic word preserves the rhyme.

132 (5.1.360–2) *Whilst . . . shroud*:   The screech-owl was regarded as
an ominous bird whose cry foretold a death.

133 (5.1.367–70) *And we . . . dream*:   This statement seems to
contradict Oberon's 'But we are fairies of another sort' (3.2.388).
'Triple Hecate' refers to the deity who was (not very consist-
ently) called Hecate or Proserpina in Hades or on earth, Diana
or Lucina on earth, and Luna, Cynthia or Phoebe in the
heavens. 'Hecate', both here and in *Macbeth*, is disyllabic: '*Heck*-
at'. The dragons pulling Hecate's chariot constituted the 'team'.

134 (5.1.373) *broom before*:   Robin Goodfellow was sometimes
described or depicted as a broom-wielder.

135 (5.1. S.D.) *OBERON* leads . . . *chorus*:   As explained earlier in this
edition, the words of the song are probably absent, and
Granville Barker filled the gap by borrowing the nuptial song
for Theseus and Hippolyta which opens *The Two Noble Kinsmen*. Here is that song.

> Roses, their sharp spines being gone,
> Not royal in their smells alone
>   But in their hue;
> Maiden pinks, of odour faint,
> Daisies smell-less, yet most quaint,
>   And sweet thyme true;
>
> Primrose, firstborn child of Ver,
> Merry Springtime's harbinger,
>   With harebells dim;
> Oxlips, in their cradles growing,
> Marigolds on deathbeds blowing,
>   Lark's-heels trim:
>
> All dear Nature's children sweet
> Lie 'fore bride and bridegroom's feet,
>   Blessing their sense.

Not an angel of the air,
Bird melodious or bird fair,
   Is absent hence.

The crow, the slanderous cuckoo, nor
The boding raven, nor chough hoar,
   Nor chattering pie,
May on our bride-house perch or sing,
Or with them any discord bring,
   But from it fly.

136 (5.1.413) *No . . . dream*: 'no more productive than a dream'.

137 (5.1.417–19) *If . . . long*: 'if, now, we have the undeserved good fortune not to be hissed by you, we shall soon improve and shall atone for our deficiencies'.

GLOSSARY

Where a pun or an ambiguity is apparent, the meanings are distinguished as (a) and (b), or (a), (b) and (c), etc. Otherwise, alternative meanings are distinguished as (i) and (ii). Abbreviations include the following: adj., adjective; vb., verb.

abide me: stay for me.
abridgement: 5.1.39: (a) 'something to wile away the time'; (b) 'short or shortened play'.
aby: 3.2.335: (a) pay the penalty for; (b) pay dearly for.
Acheron: one of the four rivers of Hades.
adamant: exceptionally hard stone or metal, the latter having magnetic powers.
addressed: 5.1.106: (a) ready; (b) costumed (and therefore ready).
admirable: wonderful.
after-supper: dessert served after supper.
against: (i: 1.1.125, 5.1.75:) in preparation for; (ii: 3.2.99:) in case.
aggravate: 1.2.71: (Bottom's error for) alleviate (moderate).
amazed: bewildered, stupefied.
an (as conjunction): if.
antic: 5.1.3: (a) ancient, antique; (b) quaint; (c) grotesque.
Antipodes: dwellers in the opposite part of the earth.
approve: 2.2.76: (a) prove; (b) test, try.
apricock: (obsolete form of) apricot.
argument: 3.2.242: topic, object (of mockery).
art: 1.1.192, 2.2.112: magical skill.
artificial: skilled in art.
attractive: magnetic.
Aurora's harbinger: Venus Phosphorus, the 'Morning Star'.
bade (pronounced 'bad'): (i) told; (ii) requested.
badge: (originally badge of a servant:) hall-mark.
bait (vb.): 3.2.197: harass, torment.
bankrout: bankrupt.
barm: yeast.
bated: excepted.
batty: bat-like.
bayed: brought to bay (by means of barking hounds).
beachèd: shingly.

Bergomask (or Bergamask):
rustic dance, sometimes
associated with Bergamo in
Italy.

berlakin: (compression of)
'by our Ladykin', i.e. 'by our
Lady, the Virgin Mary'.

beshrew: curse.

beteem: 1.1.131: (a) grant;
(b) pour down on.

bond: 3.2.267-8: (a) signed
contract; (b) fetter.

bootless (adj.): fruitless, useless.

bootless (adverb): fruitlessly, in
vain.

bottle (of hay): bundle.

bottom: (i, suggesting Bottom's
name:) core or spool on
which a weaver wound a
skein of thread or yarn;
(ii, 4.1.213:) basis, foundation.

brake: thicket of bushes.

brands: **wasted brands**: dying
embers.

brief: 5.1.42: list, summary.

bully (term of endearment):
fine fellow.

bumpkin: yokel, clumsy rural
fellow.

bur: 3.2.260: prickly seedcase
(or a person who sticks like
one).

buskined: booted, wearing
warrior's boots.

canker (noun): canker-worm,
a grub or caterpillar.

canker-blossom: grub or caterpillar that cankers a blossom.

capacity 5.1.105: understanding.

car: chariot.

carol: song sung at a festivity.

carry: (i: 3.2.240:) execute;
(ii: 5.1.225-8:) (a) sustain;
(b) carry off.

casement: that part of a window which is hinged and
opens outwards or inwards.

Cavalery (from Italian *cavaliere*):
cavalier, noble gentleman.

cheer: 3.2.96: (a) cheek;
(b) face, countenance.

chiding (noun): quarrelsome or
angry noise.

childing (adj.): fruitful,
pregnant.

chough: jackdaw.

clerks: scholars.

close (adj.): secluded, secret.

coil (noun): turmoil, quarrel.

collied: begrimed, murky.

compáct: composed.

companion (used contempt-
uously): fellow.

con: memorise.

condole: grieve, lament.

confederacy: conspiracy.

conference: conversation.

continents: 2.1.92: river-banks.

Corin: young shepherd in the
realm of pastoral amatory
poetry.

coy (vb.): caress.

crazèd: flawed.

create: 5.1.389: engendered.

crush: 3.2.366: squeeze.

cry: 4.1.123: pack (of dogs).

curst: bad-tempered.

curtsy: 4.1.20: (a) bow;
(b) courteous display.

dam: 5.1.218: animal-mother.

darkling: in the dark.

date: 3.2.373: duration.

dead: 3.2.57: (a) deadly; (b) pallid as a corpse.

defect: 3.1.34: (Bottom's error for) effect.

deflowered: 5.1.280: (Bottom's error for) devoured.

derived: descended; **as well derived**: of equally good ancestry.

desert place: deserted place.

device: play or masque for private showing.

dewberries: blackberries.

dewlap: dangling jowl: pendulous fold of skin on the throat.

die the death: suffer the death-sentence.

discharge (vb.): perform, play a part.

disfigure: 3.1.53: (Quince's error for) figure, represent.

dissembling: deceiving.

dissolved: 1.1.245: (a) broke faith; (b) melted.

distemperature: 2.1.106: (a) disorder in nature; (b) loss of temper.

dole: woe.

double tongue: forked tongue.

dove: sucking dove: 1.2.72: (Bottom's confusion of) 'sitting dove' (one sitting on eggs) and 'sucking lamb', proverbial for mildness.

dowager: stepmother or widow whose income derives from her late husband's estate.

dull: 3.2.8: drowsy.

earthlier happy: 1.1.76: (a) more fortunate on earth; (b) fortunate from a secular viewpoint.

eglantine: sweet-briar, a wild rose with pink flowers.

eight and eight: lines of eight syllables.

eight and six: alternate lines of eight and six syllables, a common ballad metre.

eke: also.

enforcèd: violated.

Ercles: 1.2.23, 34: (Bottom's version of) Hercules.

erewhile: previously.

estate unto: bestow upon.

Ethiop: ('Ethiopian':) dark-skinned African.

exeunt: they go out.

exit: he or she goes out.

exposition: 4.1.38: (Bottom's error for) disposition.

extempore: by improvisation.

extort: torture.

eyne: (then an archaic version of) eyes.

faining: 1.1.31: (a) yearning; (b) softly singing.

faint: 1.1.215: pale.

fairy time: time between midnight and dawn.

fancy (noun): (i: 1.1.155:) love, affection; (ii: 5.1.25:) imagination, fantasy; **fancy free**: uncaught by love; **fancy-sick**: love-sick; **in fancy** (4.1.162) impelled by love.

fantasy: (i: 1.1.32:) amatory imagination; (ii: 2.1.258:) extravagant fancy; **shaping fantasies**: creative imaginations.

Fates: the classical deities Clotho, Lachesis and Atropos, who allotted and ended one's life-span.

favour: (i: 2.1.12, 4.1.48:) token of love or good will; (ii: 1.1.186:) attractive face or appearance.

fee: recompense.

fell (adj.): 2.1.20, 5.1.272: (a) fierce; (b) cruel.

fie (expression of disgust): shame on you.

field-dew consecrate: sacred dew from the fields: fairies' equivalent to holy water.

flewed: i.e. with flews (flaps of skin on the jaws of a hound).

flood: 2.1.127: flowing sea.

flout: 2.2.136: scorn.

fond: 2.2.96: (a) foolish; (b) loving.

foredoone: worn out, 'done for'.

forester: warden of the forest and its animals.

forsooth: truly, indeed.

French crown: (a) the gold écu, a French coin; (b) bald head resulting from syphilis.

frolic (adj.): frolicsome, playful.

Furies: avenging spirits.

gait: **take his gait**: make his way.

gaud: trinket.

generally: 1.2.2: (Bottom's error for) individually.

glance at: cast aspersions on.

glass: 2.2.106: mirror.

gleek: make satiric jests.

go along: 1.1.123: walk beside.

gossip (noun): chattering woman.

government: **in government**: regulated, subject to control.

grace: 5.1.256: (a) graciousness; (b, punningly) grease, candle-fat.

green (noun): 2.1.99: (a) grass; (b) grassy recreation-area.

griffin: fabulous monster with the head of an eagle and the body of a lion.

grisly: hideous.

grow to a point: come to a conclusion.

guest-wise: as a temporary visitor.

harbinger: fore-runner.

Hecate: **triple Hecate's team**: the dragons pulling the chariot of the deity who was associated with the under-world, night, enchantment and witchcraft.

hempen home-spuns: people clad in home-spun cloth made of hemp: yokels.

henchman: squire or page to some important person.

Hiems (Latin): Winter (the season personified).

hight (archaic vb.): is called.

hind: female deer.

Hobgoblin: 2.1.40: normally 'mischievous fairy' but here 'fairy Rob' ('Hob' being a variant of 'Robin').

hold: 5.1.353: maintain; **hold the sweet jest up**: maintain the delightful joke.

hole: 5.1.198: (a) anus; (b) aperture.

hollowed to: yelled at.

humble-bee: bumble-bee.

humour: temperamental disposition; inclination.

i'faith: truly, indeed.

imbrue: pierce.

immediately: directly.

impeach: discredit.

increase (noun): produce of the seasons.

injurious: 3.2.195: (a) insulting; (b) unjust.

injury: 3.2.148: (a) insult; (b) injustice.

intend: 3.2.333: offer.

interlude: short play.

jangling (noun): discord, altercation.

jealousy: mistrust, suspicion.

juggler: trickster, cheat.

juvenal: juvenile.

knot-grass: *Polygonum aviculare*, a common creeping weed, an infusion of which was deemed capable of stunting a person's growth.

lanthorn (probably pronounced 'lánt-horn'): lantern.

latch (vb.): 3.2.36: (a) moisten; (b) snare.

league: 3.2.373: union; **seven leagues** (1.1.159): distance of twenty-one miles – approximately (given that, as a measure of distance, the league was variously defined as two, three and four miles).

leviathan: sea-monster; (probably) whale.

livery: uniform, distinctive garb.

lob: lout.

lode-star: star (e.g. the Pole Star) which guides navigators.

long of you: because of you.

love: **made love to**: 1.1.107: wooed (not 'copulated with').

loves: **of all loves**: 2.2.162: (a) for love's sake; (b) for the sake of all that is held dear.

maid: 2.2.67: virgin.

making (noun): 2.1.32: build, constitution.

margent: 'margin', shore.

marshal (noun): officer who arranges ceremonies and presents guests.

mask (noun): 1.2.42: veil or face-covering used by women to protect their complexions.

means (vb.): 5.1.309: moans, laments.

mechanicals: coarse workers.

mewed: caged, like a moulting hawk in its 'mew' (cage).

mimic (noun): actor.

minimus (Latin for 'least'): tiny creature.

misgraffèd: badly matched, wrongly grafted.

misprised: mistaken.

misprision: mistake.

momentany: momentary.

moon's sphere: the transparent rotating globe in which (according to the Ptolemaic system) the moon was fixed.

Moth: Mote ('Speck' or 'Tiny Person').

moused: 5.1.257: (a) seized and shaken, as a cat torments a mouse; (b) uttered quietly as a mouse.

murrion flock: diseased flock.

murther: murder.

musk-roses: wild roses with fragrant white flowers.

naught: thing of naught: 4.2.12: wicked object.

neaf: fist.

neeze: sneeze.

night-rule: 3.2.5: (a) nocturnal revels; (b) disorders.

nine men's morris: game played with nine pegs ('men'); sometimes played out of doors on a pattern cut in turf.

Ninny: mispronunciation of 'Ninus', 'ninny' meaning 'fool'.

Ninus: mythological king of Assyria and founder of Nineveh.

noll: (jocular term for) head.

obscenely: 1.2.95: (Bottom's confusion of, probably) 'obscurely' (secretly) and 'seemly' (in a seemly manner).

observation: observance.

o'erlook: 2.2.129: look upon.

o'er-shoes in: fully committed to.

oes: 3.2.188: (a) spangles; (b) circlets.

one: 'That's all one': 'That doesn't matter'.

orange-tawny: deep or dark yellow.

orbs upon the green: fairy rings.

orient pearls: precious pearls, being from oriental and not European oysters.

original (noun): 2.1.117: origin.

ounce: lynx.

overflown: overwhelmed.

over park, over pale: 'over any man-made enclosure' (a 'park' being an enclosed hunting-tract, and a 'pale' being an area of land enclosed by a fence or palings).

overwatched: stayed up too late.

owe: own, possess.

oxlip: hybrid plant, intermediate in appearance between the cowslip and the primrose.

pageant: 3.2.114: display, performance.

paramour: sexual partner, mistress.

pard: leopard.

parlous: perilous.

part: (i: 1.2.16:) rôle; (ii: 1.2.87:) player's speeches (with cues) written on strips of paper.

partition: 5.1.165: (a) wall; (b) section of a book or discourse.

parts: 3.2.153: attributes of body or character.

passing (adverb): surpassingly, exceedingly.

passion: 5.1.302: suffering, grief.

pat: (i: 3.1.2:) punctually, on cue; (ii: 5.1.183:) precisely.

patch: clown.

patched fool: clown in motley.

patent: privilege.

pavèd fountain: fountain or spring with a stony base.

peaseblossom: blossom of pea-plant.

peck (noun): quarter of a bushel, a bushel being a measure of corn equal to 8 gallons (36.4 litres).

pelting: paltry, petty.

pensioner: splendidly uni-
formed gentleman-pensioner
(like a modern Chelsea
Pensioner).

periods: 5.1.96: full stops.

perséver: persevere, persist.

pert: sprightly.

Phibbus: Phoebus Apollo, the
sun-god.

Phillida: young shepherdess in
the realm of pastoral amatory
poetry.

Philomele (Philomela): the
nightingale.

pie: magpie.

pipes of corn: simple musical
instrument made of straws.

plain-song (adj.): 3.1.119:
(a) having a simple song;
(b) with a song so simple and
repetitive as to resemble an
ecclesiastical chant.

point: (i: 2.2.127:) summit;
(ii: 5.1.118:) (a) full stop;
(b) formal detail.

preferred: 4.2.31: (a) recom-
mended; (b) chosen.

prepost'rously: topsy-turvily,
perversely.

present (vb.): perform, represent.

princess of pure white: per-
fection of whiteness.

privilege: protection, right of
immunity.

provender: dry food for animals.

puck: (a) term for a single
representative of the mischievous hobgoblins known as
pucks; (b, as **Puck**:) personal

name of such a single
representative.

purple-in-grain: permanently-
dyed blood-colour (crimson
or scarlet).

quail (vb.): 5.1.275: destroy.

quaint: (i: 2.1.99:) cunning,
ingenious; (ii: 2.2.7:) (a)
pretty, dainty; (b) unfamiliar.

quell: kill.

quern: 2.1.36: (a) churn;
(b, less likely:) handmill for
grinding corn or mustard.

questions: 2.1.235: topics for
debate.

quick: 1.1.149: (a) swift;
(b) lively.

quill: **little quill**: 3.1.116: (small
musical pipe, made of a
hollow stem; thus:) quiet
bird-song.

Quince: a name which probably derives from 'quines',
wooden wedges used by
carpenters.

rail (vb.): denounce, utter
abuse.

recorder: wooden wind-
instrument of the flute
family, held upright and
blown through a mouth-
piece at the top.

recreant: coward.

rere-mouse: bat.

respect (noun): 5.1.91: estimation, consideration; **in my
respect**: 2.1.224: (a) as far as
I am concerned; (b) in my
estimation.

respect (vb.): 1.1.160: regard.

retinue: followers.

rheumatic diseases: diseases increasing the 'rheum' (bodily fluid), including catarrhs and colds. 'Rheumatic' was normally stressed on the first syllable.

rid: 5.1.119: (a) ridden; (b) rid himself of.

ringlet: **dance our ringlets**: 2.1.86: (a) make our circling dances; (b) dance in our fairy rings.

ripe: 5.1.42: ready, fully prepared.

Robin Goodfellow: propitiatory name given to a mischievous hobgoblin or (apart from this play) a devil.

rock the ground: make the ground sway or reverberate.

rote: **by rote**: from memory.

rough-cast: wall-plaster made of lime and gravel.

round, roundel: 2.1.140, 2.2.1: country dance in which dancers form a circle; **about a round**: 3.1.97: a roundabout course..

rude: (i: 3.2.9:) coarse; (ii: 3.2.262:) uncivil.

russet: **russet-pated choughs**: russet-headed jackdaws. Russet was a drab colour ranging from reddish-brown to near-black. 'Light russet' was grey, the colour of the jackdaw's poll.

sad: 4.1.94: sober.

sanded: sandy-coloured.

saucy: impudent.

scrip: 1.2.3: (a) script (piece of writing); (b) scrap of paper.

set against: oppose.

several: separate.

shrewd: (i: 2.1.33:) mischievous; (ii: 3.2.323:) shrewish, malicious.

shroud (noun): sheet-like garment for a corpse.

simpleness: 5.1.83: (a) innocence; (b) sincerity.

simplicity: 1.1.171: (a) innocence; (b) sincerity.

since: **since night**: 3.2.275: since nightfall.

sinister: 5.1.162: left.

Sisters Three: the three Fates, who allotted life and death to mortals.

sixpence: coin or sum. Most skilled craftsmen earned between sixpence and ninepence a day.

skill: **touching the point of human skill**: 2.2.127: attaining full rationality.

Snout: the name probably derives from 'snout' meaning 'spout or nozzle'.

snuff: **in snuff**: 5.1.240: (a) smouldering and in need of wick-trimming; (b) angry.

sojourn: 3.2.171 (a) stay; (b) journey.

sort (noun): (i: 3.2.13:) set, crew; (ii: 3.2.159:) rank; **in sort**: 3.2.21: in consort, assembled.

sort (vb.): occur, come to pass.

sorting with: 5.1.55: appropriate for.

sphere: one of the transparent hollow globes in which (according to the Ptolemaic

system) the 'fixed stars'
collectively and each of the
planets were set.

spinners: long-legg'd spinners:
long-legged web-spinning
spiders.

spleen: 1.1.146: fit of bad
temper.

split: to make all split: 1.2.24:
to tear everything apart.

sport (noun): entertainment.

spotted: 1.1.110: morally
tainted.

spring (noun): 2.1.82: beginning.

spurn: 2.1.205: kick.

square (vb.): 2.1.30: quarrel.

squash (noun): unripe pea-pod.

stones: 5.1.179, 187: (a) stone
masonry; (b) testicles.

stop (noun): 5.1.120: (a) sudden
halting of a galloping horse;
(b) full stop.

streak (vb.): 2.1.257: smear.

superpraise: overpraise.

swain: 4.1.64: (a) rural youth;
(b) young lover.

'Tailor!': 2.1.54: (possibly) 'My
bum!'.

take on as: 3.2.258: pretend.

Tartar's bow: powerful doubly-
curved bow used by warriors
of Tartary.

tawny: 3.2.263: tanned, swarthy.

tear a cat: perform rantingly.

Thessalian: of Thessaly, a
mountain-bounded region of
Greece.

Thisny: (probably) pet-name
for 'Thisby'.

thorough: 2.1.3, 5: through.

throstle: thrush.

thrum: tufted end of threads left
attached to a loom when the
completed piece of cloth is
cut off.

'tide: betide, come.

tiring-house: 'attiring house':
actors' dressing-room.

tongs: pair of tongs used as a
rudimentary musical instrument, struck with a key.

touch: brave touch: fine stroke.

tóward: 3.1.70: pending.

translated: transformed.

trim (adj.): fine, neat.

troth: (i: 2.2.44:) truth;
(ii: 2.2.50:) pledge of fidelity.

Troyan: Trojan.

tunable: musical, tuneful.

unbreathed: unexercised.

urged: advocated.

vaward: vanward, forepart.

vein: 3.2.82: mood, disposition.

vilde: vile.

virtuous: 3.2.367: efficacious.

vot'ress (votaress): female
devoted, as by a vow, to some
service or order.

wanton: rash wanton: 2.1.63:
recklessly immoral female;
wanton green: 2.1.99:
(a) rank grass; (b) overgrown
grassy recreation-area.

weed: 2.1.256, 2.2.79: garment.

welkin: sky.

wend: 3.2.372: (a) turn;
(b) proceed.

wherefore: why.

whole: 3.2.53: solid.

wit: set his wit to: 3.1.122: use
his intelligence to answer.

without: 1.1.165: outside.

wood: 2.1.192: (i) mad;
(ii) wooded area.

woodbine: (i: 2.1.251:) honey-
suckle; (ii: 4.1.41:) bindweed.

woosel cock: ousel cock: male
blackbird.

worm: 3.2.71: snake.

wot: know.

wrath (adj.): 2.1.20: wrathful.

WORDSWORTH CLASSICS

REQUESTS FOR INSPECTION COPIES Lecturers wishing to obtain copies of Wordsworth Classics, Wordsworth Poetry Library or Wordsworth Classics of World Literature titles for inspection are invited to contact: Dennis Hart, Wordsworth Editions Ltd, Crib Street, Ware, Herts SG12 9ET; E-mail: dennis.hart@wordsworth-editions.com. Please quote the author, title and ISBN of the books in which you are interested, together with your name, academic address, E-mail address, the course on which the books will be used and the expected enrolment.

Teachers wishing to inspect specific core titles for GCSE or A-level courses are also invited to contact Wordsworth Editions at the above address.

Inspection copies are sent solely at the discretion of Wordsworth Editions Ltd.

JANE AUSTEN
Emma
Mansfield Park
Northanger Abbey
Persuasion
Pride and Prejudice
Sense and Sensibility

ARNOLD BENNETT
Anna of the Five Towns
The Old Wives' Tale

R. D. BLACKMORE
Lorna Doone

M. E. BRADDON
Lady Audley's Secret

ANNE BRONTË
Agnes Grey
*The Tenant of
Wildfell Hall*

CHARLOTTE BRONTË
Jane Eyre
The Professor
Shirley
Villette

EMILY BRONTË
Wuthering Heights

JOHN BUCHAN
Greenmantle
The Island of Sheep
John Macnab
Mr Standfast
The Thirty-Nine Steps
The Three Hostages

SAMUEL BUTLER
Erewhon
The Way of All Flesh

LEWIS CARROLL
Alice in Wonderland

M. CERVANTES
Don Quixote

ANTON CHEKHOV
Selected Stories

G. K. CHESTERTON
*The Club of Queer
Trades*
*Father Brown:
Selected Stories*
*The Man Who Was
Thursday*
*The Napoleon of
Notting Hill*

ERSKINE CHILDERS
The Riddle of the Sands

JOHN CLELAND
*Fanny Hill – Memoirs of
a Woman of Pleasure*

WILKIE COLLINS
The Moonstone
The Woman in White

JOSEPH CONRAD
Almayer's Folly
Heart of Darkness
Lord Jim
Nostromo
Sea Stories
The Secret Agent
Selected Short Stories
Victory

J. FENIMORE COOPER
The Last of the Mohicans

STEPHEN CRANE
The Red Badge of Courage

THOMAS DE QUINCEY
*Confessions of an English
Opium Eater*

DANIEL DEFOE
Moll Flanders
Robinson Crusoe

CHARLES DICKENS
Barnaby Rudge
Bleak House
Christmas Books
David Copperfield
Dombey and Son
Best Ghost Stories
Great Expectations
Hard Times
Little Dorrit
Martin Chuzzlewit
The Mystery of Edwin Drood
Nicholas Nickleby
The Old Curiosity Shop
Oliver Twist
Our Mutual Friend
The Pickwick Papers
Sketches by Boz
A Tale of Two Cities

BENJAMIN DISRAELI
Sybil

FYODOR DOSTOEVSKY
Crime and Punishment
The Idiot

ARTHUR CONAN DOYLE
*The Adventures of
Sherlock Holmes*
The Best of Sherlock Holmes
*The Case-Book of
Sherlock Holmes*
*The Hound of the
Baskervilles*
*The Return of
Sherlock Holmes*
*The Lost World &
Other Stories*
Sir Nigel
*A Study in Scarlet &
The Sign of The Four*
Tales of Unease
The Valley of Fear
The White Company